The Seven Sayings *of the* Saviour *on the* Cross

Arthur W. Pink

BakerBooks

Grand Rapids, Michigan

Foreword © Baker Book House

Published by Baker Books
a division of Baker Publishing Group
P.O. Box 6287, Grand Rapids, MI 49516-6287
www.bakerbooks.com

New paperback edition published 2005

Previously published in 1984

Printed in the United States of America

Library of Congress Cataloging-in-Publication Data
Pink, Arthur Walkington, 1886–1952.
    The seven sayings of the Saviour on the cross / Arthur W. Pink. — New pbk. ed.
        p.   cm.
    Originally published: 1984.
    Includes indexes.
    ISBN 10: 0-8010-6573-9 (pbk.)
    ISBN 978-0-8010-6573-6 (pbk.)
    1. Jesus Christ—Crucifixion. 2. Jesus Christ—Seven last words. I. Title.
BT457.P5 2005
232.96'35—dc22   2005013246

Unless otherwise indicated, Scripture is taken from the King James Version of the Bible.

Scripture marked RSV is taken from the Revised Standard Version of the Bible, copyright 1952 [2nd edition, 1971] by the Division of Christian Education of the National Council of the Churches of Christ in the United States of America. Used by permission. All rights reserved.

18   19   20   21   22   23   15   14   13   12   11   10

The Seven Sayings
of the Saviour
on the Cross

Contents

Foreword

by Warren W. Wiersbe

When I began my ministry over fifty years ago, like many other ministers of my generation I found great help in the books of Arthur W. Pink. His reverence for God's Word, his desire to exalt Jesus Christ, and his emphasis on practical obedience all helped to keep me balanced in the study, in the pulpit, and in my personal life.

"Unless our 'Bible study' is conforming us, both inwardly and outwardly, to the image of Christ," Pink wrote, "it profits us not." He told his close friends that his articles in his publication *Studies in Scripture* were "hammered out on the anvil of [his] own heart." He carried on that publication for many years, always trusting the Lord to provide the needed finances, and he claimed that he had read over a million pages of theological literature as he prepared his messages and articles. It was clear that he had a special love for the old Puritan divines. "Mr. Pink is a Puritan in reality," said his wife, "and often says to me that he is 200 or 300 years out of his time." Yet he was consistently very contemporary as he applied the Word.

Pink taught us to have faith in the Scriptures. "Do your duty where God has stationed you," he counseled his readers. "Plough up the fallow ground and sow the seed; and though there be no fruit in your day, who knows but what an Elisha may follow you and do the reaping."

During my years of pastoral and radio ministry, I often preached messages based on the seven sayings of Jesus from the cross. I have found this volume very helpful, and I know it has been instructing and encouraging Christians for decades. Pink has a way of keeping the text in context, relating it to parallel texts, explaining it, and then applying it to everyday life.

He died in 1952, and his last words were, "The Scriptures explain themselves." I am grateful that he left behind many books that have helped us grasp the truth of that testimony.

Foreword

by John MacArthur

Arthur Pink was a master of biblical exposition, carefully mining the biblical text for every ounce of true meaning, every nuance of doctrine, and every point of personal application he could discover. He always wrote with heartfelt conviction and persuasive insight. He was warm and positive yet bold and unequivocal.

This volume has long been one of my favorite works from Pink's pen. He was at his best whenever he wrote about Christ, and he was never more focused, more thorough, or more compelling than when he proclaimed Christ crucified. In this book, he expounds the meaning of the cross through the last words of the Savior Himself. These are deeply moving glimpses of Christ in His extremity. Every chapter is a treasure.

Pink's approach is a masterful blend of literary and sermonic styles. He expounds each of the seven last sayings of Christ in seven points, all drawn straight from the biblical text. The gospel is plainly expounded throughout, so this book is a good way to introduce unbelievers to the true meaning of Christ's sufferings. But there's also enough substance here to satisfy anyone's spiritual appetite.

The Seven Sayings of the Saviour on the Cross is now nearly fifty years old—and timelier than ever. Public interest in the story of the crucifixion is approaching an all-time high, thanks to a spate of recent films, books, and television programs on the subject.

At the same time, however, many Christians today seem terribly confused about the *meaning* of the crucifixion. We occasionally hear evangelical leaders wondering out loud if the doctrine of substitutionary atonement is simply too medieval for this postmodern era. Some have even complained that it seems overly harsh to teach that Christ suffered to pay the penalty of sin—and that He did so in obedience to His Father's will. At least one popular Christian book has likened the idea to "cosmic child abuse."

Arthur Pink would have been appalled. He had no such artificial scruples. He certainly had no wish to tone down the offense of the cross just to accommodate the tastes of contemporary culture. His chapter on "The Word of Anguish" (explaining why Jesus cried out to His Father, "Why hast thou forsaken me?") is a masterpiece of clarity and candor. It is the kind of straightforward teaching that is desperately needed in an era when difficult biblical truths are sometimes purposely softened, made foggy, or revised to suit the gentle preferences of sophisticated postmodernity. Arthur Pink would have none of that. Nor should we (see 1 Cor. 2:1–5; Gal. 1:10).

You cannot read *The Seven Sayings of the Saviour on the Cross* and come away confused about the meaning of the cross or untouched by the pathos and power of Christ's death in the place of sinners. Here is an ideal antidote to some of the superficiality and silliness of today's prevailing spiritual climate.

I'm very grateful to see this book in a new edition and hopeful that it will be used by God to awaken a generation of readers to the real significance of what Christ said and what He accomplished—especially the eternal victory He won for sinners—during those dark hours while He hung on the cross.

Introduction

The death of the Lord Jesus Christ is a subject of never-failing interest to all who study prayerfully the Scripture of Truth. This is so not only because the believer's all, both for time and eternity, depends upon it, but also because of its transcendent uniqueness. Four words appear to sum up the salient features of this Mystery of mysteries: The Death of Christ was natural, unnatural, preternatural, and supernatural. A few comments seem called for by way of definition and amplification.

First, the Death of Christ was *natural*. By this we mean that it was a *real* death. It is because we are so familiar with the fact of it that the above statement appears simple and commonplace, yet what we here touch upon is to the spiritual mind one of the main elements of wonderment. The One who was "taken, and by wicked hands" crucified and slain was none less than Immanuel. The One who died on Calvary's Cross was none other than Jehovah's "Fellow." The blood that was shed on the accursed Tree was Divine—"The church of God, which *he* hath purchased with *his own* blood" (Acts 20:28, emphasis added). As says the apostle, "*God was in Christ*, reconciling the world unto himself" (2 Cor. 5:19, emphasis added). But how could Jehovah's "Fellow" *suffer*? How could the Eternal

One *die*? Ah, He who in the beginning was the Word, who was with God, and who was God, *"became flesh."* He who was in the form of God took upon Him the form of a servant and was made in the likeness of men; "and being found in fashion as a man, he humbled himself, and became obedient unto death, even the death of the cross" (Phil. 2:8). Thus having become incarnate, the Lord of Glory was capable of suffering death, and so it was that He "tasted" death itself. In His words, "Father, into thy hands I commend my spirit" we see how natural His death was, and the reality of it became still more apparent when He was laid in the tomb, where He remained for three days.

Second, the Death of Christ was *un-natural*. By this we mean that it was *abnormal*. Above we have said that in becoming incarnate, the Son of God became capable of suffering death, yet it must not be inferred from this that death therefore had a claim upon Him; far from this being the case, the very reverse was the truth. Death is the wages of sin, and He had none. Before His birth it was said to Mary, "that holy thing which shall be born of thee shall be called the Son of God" (Luke 1:35). Not only did the Lord Jesus enter this world without contracting the defilement attaching to *fallen* human nature, but He "did no sin" (1 Pet. 2:22), had "no sin" (1 John 3:5), "knew no sin" (2 Cor. 5:21). In His person and in His conduct, He was the Holy One of God "without blemish and without spot" (1 Pet. 1:19). As such, death *had no claim* upon Him. Even Pilate had to acknowledge that he could find in Him "no fault." Hence we say, for the Holy One of God to *die* was *un-natural*.

Third, the Death of Christ was *preter-natural*. By this we mean that it was marked out and *determined for Him beforehand*. He was the Lamb slain from the foundation of the world (Rev. 13:8). Before Adam was created, the Fall was anticipated. Before sin entered the world, salvation from it had been planned by God. In the eternal counsels of Deity, it was foreordained that there should be a Saviour for sinners, a Saviour who should suffer the just for the unjust, a Saviour who should die in order that we might live. And "because there was none other good enough to pay the price of sin" the only Begotten of the Father offered Himself as the Ransom.

The preternatural character of the Death of Christ has been well termed the "*undergirding* of the Cross." It was in view of that approaching Death that God justly "passed over former sins" (Rom. 3:25 RSV). Had not Christ been, in the reckoning of God, the Lamb slain from the foundation of the world, every sinning person in Old Testament times would have gone down to the Pit the moment he sinned!

Fourth, the Death of Christ was *super-natural*. By this we mean that it was *different from every other death*. In all things He has the preeminence. His birth was different from all other births. His life was different from all other lives. And His death was different from all other deaths. This was clearly intimated in His own utterance upon the subject—"Therefore doth my Father love me, because *I lay down my life*, that I might take it again. *No man taketh it from me*, but I lay it down myself. I have power to . . . take it again" (John 10:17–18, emphasis added). A careful study of the Gospel narratives that *describe* His death furnish a *sevenfold proof* and verification of His assertion.

1. That our Lord "laid down his life," that He was *not* powerless in the hands of His enemies comes out clearly in John 18, where we have the record of His *arrest*. A band of officers from the chief priests and Pharisees, headed by Judas, sought Him in Gethsemane. Coming forward to meet them, the Lord Jesus asks, "Whom seek ye?" The reply was, "Jesus of Nazareth," and then our Lord uttered the ineffable title of Deity, that by which Jehovah had revealed Himself of old to Moses at the burning bush—"I am." The effect was startling. We are told "they went backward, and fell to the ground." These officers were awestruck. They were in the presence of incarnate Deity and were overpowered by a brief consciousness of Divine majesty. How plain it is then that had He so pleased,

our blessed Saviour could have walked quietly away, leaving those who had come to arrest Him prostrate on the ground! Instead, He delivers Himself up into their hands and is *led* (not driven) as a lamb to the slaughter.

2. Let us now turn to Matthew 27:46—the most solemn verse in all the Bible—"And about the ninth hour Jesus cried *with a loud voice*, saying, Eli, Eli, lama sabachthani? that is to say, My God, my God, why hast thou forsaken me?" The words that we would ask the reader to observe carefully are here placed in italics. Why is it that the Holy Spirit tells us that the Saviour uttered that terrible cry "with a loud voice"? Most certainly there is a reason for it. This becomes even more apparent when we note that He has repeated these words four verses lower down in the same chapter—"Jesus, when he had cried *again with a loud voice*, yielded up the ghost" (Matt. 27:50, emphasis added). What then do these words indicate? Do they not *corroborate* what has been said in the above paragraphs? Do they not tell us that the Saviour *was not exhausted* by what He had passed through? Do they not intimate that His strength had not failed Him? that He was still master of Himself, that instead of being conquered by death, He was but yielding Himself to it? Do they not show us that God *had* "laid help upon one that was mighty" (Ps. 89:19)?

3. We call attention next to His fourth utterance on the Cross—" I thirst." This word, in the light of its setting, furnishes a wonderful evidence of our Lord's complete self-possession. The whole verse reads as follows: "After this, Jesus knowing that all things were now accomplished, *that the scripture might be fulfilled*, saith, I thirst" (John 19:28, emphasis added). Of old it had been predicted that they should give the Saviour to drink vinegar mingled with gall. And in order that this prophecy might be fulfilled, He cried, "I thirst." How this evidences the fact that He was in full possession of His mental faculties, that His mind was unclouded, that His terrible sufferings had neither deranged nor disturbed it. As He hung on the Cross, at the *close* of the six hours, His mind reviewed the entire

scope of the prophetic word and checked off one by one those predictions that had reference to His passion. Excepting the prophecies that were to be fulfilled *after* His death, but one remained *un*fulfilled, namely, "They gave me also gall for my meat; and in my thirst they gave me vinegar to drink" (Ps. 69:21), and this was not overlooked by the blessed Sufferer. "Jesus *knowing all things* were now accomplished, that the scripture [not "Scriptures," the reference being to Ps. 69:21] might be fulfilled, saith, I thirst." Again, we say, what proof is here furnished that He "laid down his life of *himself*"!

4. The next verification the Holy Spirit has supplied of our Lord's words in John 10:18 is found in John 19:30—"When Jesus therefore had received the vinegar, he said, It is finished: and *he bowed his head*, and gave up the ghost" (emphasis added). What are we intended to learn from these words? What is here signified by this act of the Saviour? Surely the answer is not far to seek. The implication is clear. *Previous to this*, our Lord's head had been *held erect*. It was no impotent sufferer that hung there in a swoon. Had that been the case, His *head* had lolled helplessly on His chest, and it would have been impossible for Him to "bow" it. And mark attentively the verb used here: it is not His head "fell," but He—consciously, calmly, reverently—*bowed* His head. How sublime was His carriage even on the Tree! What superb composure did He evidence. Was it not *His majestic* bearing on the Cross that, among other things, caused the centurion to cry "Truly this was the Son of God" (Matt. 27:54)!

5. Look now at His last act of all: "And when Jesus had cried with a loud voice, he said, Father, into thy hands I *commend my spirit*: and having said thus, *he gave up* the ghost" (Luke 23:46, emphasis added). None else ever did this or died thus. How accurately these words agree with His own statement, so often quoted by us, "I lay down my life, that I might take it again. No man taketh it from me, but *I lay it down of myself*" (John 10:17–18, emphasis added). The uniqueness of our Lord's action may be seen by comparing His words on the Cross with

those of dying Stephen. As the first Christian martyr came to the brink of the river, he cried, "Lord Jesus, receive my spirit" (Acts 7:59). But in contrast with this, Christ said, "Father, into thy hands *I commend* my spirit." Stephen's spirit was being *taken from him*. Not so with the Saviour. None could take from Him *His* life. He "gave up" His spirit.

6. The action of the soldiers in regard to the legs of those on the three crosses gives further evidence of the uniqueness of Christ's death. We read, "The Jews therefore, because it was the preparation, that the bodies should not remain upon the cross on the Sabbath day (for that Sabbath day was an high day), besought Pilate that their legs might be broken, and that they might be taken away. Then came the soldiers, and brake the legs of the first, and of the other which was crucified with him. But when they came to Jesus, and saw that he was dead already, they brake not his legs" (John 19:31–33). The Lord Jesus said the two thieves had been crucified together. They had been on their respective crosses the same length of time. And now at the close of the day the two thieves were still alive, for as it is well known death by crucifixion, though exceedingly painful, was usually a slow death. No vital member of the body was directly affected and often the sufferer lingered on for two or three days before being completely overcome by exhaustion. It was not natural, therefore, that Christ should be dead after but six hours on the Cross. The Jews recognized this and requested Pilate that the legs of all three be broken and death be thus hastened. In the fact, then, that the Saviour *was* "dead already" when the soldiers came to Him, though the two thieves yet lived, we have additional proof that He had voluntarily "laid down his life of himself," that it was not "taken from him."

7. For the final demonstration of the *super-natural* character of Christ's death, we turn to note the wonderful phenomena that accompanied it, "And, behold, the veil of the temple was rent in twain from the top to the bottom; and the earth did quake, and the rocks rent; and the graves were opened"

16

(Matt. 27:51–52). That was no ordinary death that had been witnessed on the summit of Golgotha's rugged heights, and it was followed by no ordinary attendants. First, the veil of the temple was rent in twain from top to bottom, to show that a Hand from heaven had torn asunder that curtain that shut out the temple worshipper from the earthly throne of God—thus signifying that the way into the Holiest was now made plain and that access to God Himself had been opened up through the broken body of His Son. Next, the earth did quake. Not, I believe, that there was *an* earthquake, nor even a "great earthquake," but the earth itself, the entire earth was shaken to its very foundation and rocked on its axis, as though to show it was horrified at the most awful deed that had ever been perpetrated on its surface. "And the rocks rent"—the very strength of Nature gave way before the greater power of that Death. Finally, we are told, "the graves were opened," showing that the power of Satan, which is death, was there shivered and shattered—all the outward attestations of the *value* of that atoning death.

Putting these together: the manifest yielding up of Himself into the hands of those who arrested Him; the crying with a "loud voice," denoting His retained vigor; the fact that He was in full and unimpaired possession of His mentality, evidenced by the "knowing that all things were now accomplished"; the "bowing" of the erect head; the deliberate "committing" of His spirit into the hands of the Father; the fact that He was "dead already" when the soldiers came to break His legs—all furnished proof that His life *was not* "taken from him," but that He laid it down of Himself and this, together with the tearing of the temple veil, the quaking of the earth, the rending of the rocks, and the opening of the graves, all bore unmistakable witness to the *super-natural* character of His death; in view of which we may well say with the wondering centurion, "Truly this was the Son of God."

The Death of Christ, then, was unique, miraculous, supernatural. In the chapters that follow we shall hearken to the words that fell from His lips while He hung upon the Cross—words that make known to us some of the attendant circumstances of the great Tragedy; words that reveal the excellencies of the One who suffered there; words in which is wrapped up the Gospel of our Salvation; and words that inform us of the purpose, the meaning, the sufferings, and the sufficiency of the Death Divine.

1

The Word of Forgiveness

Then said Jesus, Father, forgive them; for they know not
what they do.

Luke 23:34

Man had done his worst. The One by whom the world was
made had come into it, but the world knew Him not. The Lord
of Glory had tabernacled among men, but He was not wanted.
The eyes that sin had blinded saw in Him no beauty that He
should be desired. At His birth there was no room in the inn,
which foreshadowed the treatment He was to receive at the
hands of men. Shortly after His birth, Herod sought to slay
Him, and this intimated the hostility His person evoked and
forecast the Cross as the climax of man's enmity. Again and
again His enemies attempted His destruction. And now their
vile desires are granted them. The Son of God had yielded Himself up into their hands. A mock trial had been gone through,
and though His judges found no fault in Him, nevertheless,
they had yielded to the insistent clamoring of those who hated
Him as they cried again and again, "Crucify him."

The fell deed had been done. No ordinary death would suffice His implacable foes. A death of intense suffering and shame was decided upon. A cross had been secured; the Saviour had been nailed to it. And there He hangs—silent. But presently His pallid lips are seen to move—Is He crying for pity? No. What then? Is He pronouncing malediction upon His crucifiers? No. He is praying, praying for His enemies—"Then said Jesus, Father, forgive them; for they know not what they do" (Luke 23:34).

This first of the seven cross sayings of our Lord presents Him in the attitude of *prayer*. How significant! How instructive! His public ministry had opened with prayer (Luke 3:21), and here we see it closing in prayer. Surely He has left us an example! No longer might those hands minister to the sick, for they are nailed to the Cross; no longer may those feet carry Him on errands of mercy, for they are fastened to the cruel Tree; no longer may He engage in instructing the apostles, for they have forsaken Him and fled—how then does He occupy Himself? In the Ministry of Prayer! What a lesson for us.

Perhaps these lines may be read by some who by reason of age and sickness are no longer able to work actively in the Lord's vineyard. Possibly in days gone by, you were a teacher, you were a preacher, a Sunday school teacher, a tract distributor; but now you are bedridden. Yes, but you are still here on earth! Who knows but what God is leaving you here a few more days to engage in the Ministry of Prayer—and perhaps accomplish *more* by this than by all your past active service. If you are tempted to *disparage* such a ministry, remember your Saviour. *He* prayed, prayed for others, prayed for sinners, *even in His last hours*.

In praying for His enemies, not only did Christ set before us a perfect example of how we should treat those who wrong and hate us, but He also taught us never to regard any as *beyond* the reach of prayer. If Christ prayed for His murderers, then surely we have encouragement to pray now for the very chief of sinners! Christian reader, *never lose hope*. Does it seem a waste of time for you to *continue* praying for that man, that woman, that wayward child of yours? Does *their* case seem to become more hopeless every day? Does it look as though they had gotten *beyond* the reach of Divine mercy? Perhaps that one you have prayed for so long has been ensnared by one of the Satanic cults of the day, or he may now be an avowed and blatant infidel, in a word, an open enemy of Christ. Remember then the Cross. *Christ* prayed for His *enemies*. Learn, then, not to look on any as *beyond* the reach of prayer.

One other thought concerning this prayer of Christ. We are shown here the *efficacy* of prayer. This cross intercession of Christ for His enemies met with a marked and definite answer. The answer is seen in the conversion of the three thousand souls on the Day of Pentecost. I base this conclusion on Acts 3:17 where the apostle Peter says, "And now, brethren, I wot that through ignorance ye did it, as did also your rulers." It is to be noted that Peter uses the word "ignorance," which corresponds with our Lord's "they know not what they do." Here, then, is the divine explanation of the three thousand converted under a single sermon. It was not Peter's eloquence that was the cause but the Saviour's prayer. And, Christian reader, the same is true of us. Christ prayed for you and me long before we believed in Him. Turn to John 17:20 for proof. "Neither pray I for these [the apostles] alone, but for them also *which shall believe on me* through their word" (John 17:20, emphasis added). Once more let us profit from the perfect Exemplar. Let us too make intercession for the enemies of God, and if we pray in faith, we also shall pray effectively unto the salvation of lost sinners.

To come now directly to our text: "Then said Jesus, Father, forgive them; for they know not what they do."

1. Here we see the fulfillment of the prophetic word.

How much God made known beforehand of what should transpire on that day of days! What a complete picture did the Holy Spirit furnish of our Lord's passion with all the attendant

21

circumstances! Among other things it had been foretold that the Saviour should make "intercession for the transgressors" (Isa. 53:12). This did not have reference to the present ministry of Christ at God's right hand. It is true that "he is able also to save them to the uttermost that come unto God by him, seeing he ever liveth to make intercession for them" (Heb. 7:25), but this speaks of what He is doing now for those who have believed on Him, whereas Isaiah 53:12 had reference to His gracious act at the time of His crucifixion. Observe what His intercession for the transgressors is there linked with—"And he was numbered with the transgressors; and he bare the sin of many, and made intercession for the transgressors."

That Christ should make intercession for His enemies was one of the items of the wonderful prophecy found in Isaiah 53. This chapter tells us at least ten things about the humiliation and suffering of the Redeemer. It declared that He should be despised and rejected of men; that He should be a man of sorrows and acquainted with grief; that He should be wounded, bruised, and chastised; that He should be led, unresistingly, to slaughter; that He should be dumb before His shearers; that He should not only suffer at the hands of man but also be bruised by the Lord; that He should pour out His soul unto death; that He should be buried in a rich man's tomb; and then it was added, that He would be numbered with transgressors; and finally, that He should make intercession for the transgressors. Here then was the prophecy—"and made intercession for the transgressors"; there was the fulfillment of it—"Father, forgive them; for they know not what they do." He thought of His murderers; He pleaded for His crucifiers; He made intercession for their forgiveness.

"Then said Jesus, Father, forgive them; for they know not what they do."

2. Here we see Christ identified with His people.

"Father, forgive them." On no previous occasion did Christ make such a request of the Father. Never before had He involved the Father's forgiveness of others. Hitherto *He forgave* Himself. To the man sick of the palsy, He had said, "Son, be of good cheer; thy sins be forgiven thee" (Matt. 9:2). To the woman who washed His feet with her tears in the house of Simon, He said, "Thy sins are forgiven" (Luke 7:48). Why, then, should He now ask *the Father* to forgive, instead of directly pronouncing forgiveness Himself?

Forgiveness of sin is a *Divine* prerogative. The Jewish scribes were right when they reasoned "Who can forgive sins but God only?" (Mark 2:7). But you say, Christ was God. Truly, but Man also—the God-man. He was the Son of God who had become the Son of Man with the express purpose of offering Himself as a Sacrifice for sin. And when the Lord Jesus cried "*Father, forgive* them," He was on the Cross, and *there* He might not exercise His divine prerogatives. Mark carefully His own words, and then behold the marvelous accuracy of Scripture. He had said, "The Son of man hath power on *earth* to forgive sins" (Matt. 9:6, emphasis added). But He was no longer on earth! He had been "lifted up *from the earth*" (John 12:32, emphasis added). Moreover, on the Cross He was acting as our substitute: the just was about to die for the unjust. Hence it was that hanging there as our representative, He was *no longer in the place of authority* where He might exercise His own divine prerogatives, therefore takes He the position of a *suppliant* before the Father. Thus we say that when the blessed Lord Jesus cried, "*Father, forgive them*," we see Him absolutely *identified with His people*. No longer was He in the position "on earth" where He had the "power" or "right" to forgive sins; instead, He *intercedes* for sinners—as we must.

"Then said Jesus, Father, forgive them; *for they know not what they do.*"

3. Here we see the divine estimate of sin and its consequent guilt.

Under the Levitical economy God required that atonement should be made for sins of ignorance. "If a soul commit a trespass, *and sin through ignorance*, in the holy things of the LORD; then he shall bring for his trespass unto the LORD a ram without blemish out of the flocks, with thy estimation by shekels of silver, after the shekel of the sanctuary, for a trespass offering: and he shall make amends for the harm that he hath done in the holy thing, and shall add the fifth part thereto, and give it unto the priest: and the priest shall *make an atonement for him* with the ram of the trespass offering, and it shall be forgiven him" (Lev. 5:15–16, emphasis added). And again we read, "And if ye have erred, and not observed all these commandments, which the LORD hath spoken unto Moses, even all that the LORD hath commanded you by the hand of Moses, from the day that the LORD commanded Moses, and henceforward among your generations; then it shall be, if aught be committed *by ignorance* without the knowledge of the congregation, that all the congregation shall offer one young bullock for a burnt offering, for a sweet savour unto the LORD, with his meat offering, and his drink offering, according to the manner, and one kid of the goats for a sin offering. And the priest shall make an atonement for all the congregation of the children of Israel, and it shall be forgiven them; for it is ignorance: and they shall bring their offering, a sacrifice made by fire unto the LORD, *and their sin offering* before the LORD, *for their ignorance*" (Num. 15:22–25, emphasis added). It is in view of such Scriptures as these that we find David prayed, "Cleanse thou me from *secret* faults" (Ps. 19:12, emphasis added).

Sin is always sin in the sight of God, whether we are conscious of it or not. Sins of ignorance need atonement just as truly as do conscious sins. God is Holy, and He will not lower His standard of righteousness to the level of our ignorance. Ignorance is not innocence. As a matter of fact, ignorance is more culpable now than it was in the days of Moses. We have no excuse for our ignorance. God has clearly and fully revealed His will. The Bible is in our hands, and we cannot plead ignorance of its contents except to condemn our laziness. God has spoken, and by His Word we shall be judged.

And yet the fact remains that we *are* ignorant of many things, and the fault and blame are ours. And this does not minimize the enormity of our guilt. Sins of ignorance need the divine forgiveness as our Lord's prayer here plainly shows. Learn, then, how high is God's standard, how great is our need, and praise Him for an atonement of infinite sufficiency, which cleanseth from *all* sin.

"Then said Jesus, Father, forgive them; *for they know not what they do.*"

4. Here we see the blindness of the human heart.

"They know not what they do." This does not mean that the enemies of Christ were ignorant of the *fact* of His crucifixion. They did know full well that they had cried out "Crucify him." They did know full well that their vile request had been granted them by Pilate. They did know full well that He had been nailed to the Tree, for they were eyewitnesses of the crime. What, then, did our Lord mean when He said, "They know not what they do"? He meant they were ignorant of the *enormity* of their crime. They "knew not" that it was the Lord of Glory they were crucifying. The emphasis is not on "they *know not*" but on "they know not *what* they do."

And yet they *ought* to have known. Their blindness was inexcusable. The Old Testament prophecies that had received their fulfillment in Him were sufficiently plain to identify Him as the Holy One of God. His teaching was unique, for His very critics were forced to admit "Never man spake like this man" (John 7:46). And what of His perfect life! He had lived before men a life that had never been lived on earth before. He pleased not Himself. He went about doing good. He was ever at the disposal of others. There was no self-seeking about Him. His was a life of self-sacrifice from beginning to end. His was a life ever lived to the glory of God. His was a life on which was stamped Heaven's approval, for the Father's voice testified audibly "This is my beloved Son, in whom I am *well pleased.*" No, there was no excuse for their ignorance. It only demonstrated the blindness of their hearts. Their rejection of the Son of God bore full witness, once for all, that the carnal mind *is* "enmity against God."

How sad to think this terrible tragedy is still being repeated! Sinner, you little know what you are doing in neglecting God's great salvation. You little know how awful is the sin of slighting the Christ of God and spurning the invitations of His mercy. You little know the deep guilt that is attached to your act of refusing to receive the only One who can save you from your sins. You little know how fearful is the crime of saying, "We will not have this man to reign over us." You know not what you do. You regard the vital issue with callous indifference. The question comes today as it did of old, "What shall I do with Jesus which is called Christ?" for you *have* to do something with Him: either you despise and reject Him, or you receive Him as the Saviour of your soul and the Lord of your life. But, I say again, it seems to you a matter of small moment, of little importance, *which* you do. For years you have resisted the strivings of His Spirit. For years you have shelved the all-important consideration. For years you have steeled your heart against Him, closed your ears to His appeals, and shut your eyes to His surpassing beauty. Ah! *you know not WHAT you do.* You are blind to your madness. Blind to your terrible sin. Yet are you not *excuseless.* You may be saved now if you will. "Believe on the Lord Jesus Christ, and *thou* shalt be saved." O come to the Saviour now and say with one of old, "Lord, that I might receive my sight."

"Then said Jesus, Father, *forgive them*; for they know not what they do."

5. Here we see a lovely exemplification of His own teaching.

In the Sermon on the Mount our Lord taught His disciples, "Love your enemies, bless them that curse you, do good to them that hate you, and pray for them which despitefully use you, and persecute you" (Matt. 5:44). Above all others Christ practiced what He preached. Grace *and truth* came by Jesus Christ. He

26

not only taught the truth but was Himself the truth incarnate. Said He, "I am the way, the truth, and the life" (John 14:6). So here on the Cross He perfectly exemplified His teaching of the mount. In all things He has left us an example.

Notice Christ did not *personally* forgive His enemies. So in Matthew 5:44, He did not exhort His disciples to forgive their enemies, but He *does* exhort them to "pray" for them. But are *we* not to forgive those who wrong us? This leads us to a point concerning which there is much need for instruction today. Does Scripture teach that under all circumstances we must always forgive? I answer emphatically, it does not. The Word of God says, "If thy brother trespass against thee, rebuke him; and *if he repent*, forgive him. And if he trespass against thee seven times a day, and seven times in a day turn again to thee, saying, *I repent*; thou shalt forgive him" (Luke 17:3–4, emphasis added). Here we are plainly taught that a condition must be met by the offender *before* we may pronounce forgiveness. The one who has wronged us must first "repent," that is, judge himself for his wrong and give evidence of his sorrow over it. But suppose the offender does not repent? Then I am not to forgive him. But let there be no misunderstanding of our meaning here. Even though the one who has wronged me does not repent, nevertheless, I must not harbor ill feelings against him. There must be no hatred or malice cherished in the heart. Yet, on the other hand, I must not treat the offender as if he had done no wrong. That would be to condone the offense, and therefore I should fail to uphold the requirements of righteousness, and this the believer is ever to do. Does *God* ever forgive where there is no repentance? No, for Scripture declares, "*If we confess our sins*, he is faithful and just to forgive us our sins, and to cleanse us from all unrighteousness" (1 John 1:9, emphasis added). One thing more. If one has injured me and repented not, while I cannot forgive him and treat him as though he had not offended, nevertheless, not only must I hold no malice in my heart against him, but I must also *pray for him.* Here is the value of Christ's perfect example. If we cannot forgive, we can pray for God to forgive him.

"Then said Jesus, Father, forgive them; for they know not what they do."

6. Here we see man's great and primary need.

The first important lesson that all need to learn is that we are sinners, and as such, *unfit* for the presence of a Holy God. It is in vain that we select noble ideals, form good resolutions, and adopt excellent rules to live by, until the sin question has been settled. It is of no avail that we attempt to develop a beautiful character and aim to do that which will meet with God's approval while there is sin between Him and our souls. Of what use are shoes if our feet are paralyzed? Of what use are glasses if we are blind? The question of the forgiveness of my sins is basic, fundamental, vital. It matters not that I am highly respected by a wide circle of friends if I am yet in my sins. It matters not that I have made good in business if I am an unpardoned transgressor in the sight of God. What *will* matter most in the hour of death is, Have my sins been put away by the Blood of Christ?

The second all-important lesson that all need to learn is how forgiveness of sins may be obtained. What is the *ground* on which a Holy God will forgive sins? And here it is important to remark that there is a vital difference between divine forgiveness and much of human forgiveness. As a general rule, human forgiveness is a matter of leniency, often of laxity. We mean forgiveness is shown at the expense of justice and righteousness. In a human court of law, the judge has to choose between two alternatives: when the one in the dock has been proven guilty, the judge must either *enforce* the penalty of the law, or he must *disregard* the requirements of the law—the one is justice, the other is mercy. The only possible way by which the judge can both enforce the requirements of the law and yet show mercy to its offender is by a third party offering to suffer in his own person the penalty that the convicted one deserves. Thus it was in the divine counsels, God would not exercise mercy at the expense of justice. God, as the judge of all the earth, would not set aside the demands of His Holy law. Yet God would show mercy. How? Through one making full satisfaction to His outraged law. Through His own Son taking the place of all those who believe on Him and bearing their sins in His own body on the tree. God could be just and yet merciful, merciful and yet just. Thus it is that "grace reigns *through righteousness.*"

A righteous ground has been provided on which God can be *just* and yet the justifier of all who believe. Hence it is we are told, "Thus it is written, and thus it behooved Christ to suffer, and to rise from the dead the third day: and that repentance and remission [forgiveness] of sins should be preached in his name among all nations, beginning at Jerusalem" (Luke 24:46–47). And again, "Be it known unto you therefore, men and brethren, that through this man is preached unto you the forgiveness of sins: and by him all that believe are justified from all things, from which ye could not be justified by the law of Moses" (Acts 13:38–39). It was in view of the blood He was shedding that the Saviour cried, "Father, forgive them." It was in view of the atoning sacrifice He was offering, that it can be said, "Without shedding of blood is no remission."

In praying for the *forgiveness* of His enemies, Christ struck right down to the root of their *need.* And their need was the need of every child of Adam. Reader, have *your* sins been forgiven? that is, remitted or sent away. Are you, by grace, one of those of whom it is said, "In whom we have redemption through his blood, even the forgiveness of sins" (Col. 1:14)?

"*Then* said Jesus, Father, forgive them; for they know not what they do."

7. Here we see the triumph of redeeming love.

Mark closely the word with which our text opens: "Then." The verse that immediately precedes it reads thus, "And when they were come to the place, which is called Calvary, there

29

they crucified him, and the malefactors, one on the right hand, and the other on the left" (Luke 23:33). *Then*, said Jesus, Father, forgive them. "Then"—when man had done his worst. "Then"—when the vileness of the human heart was displayed in climacteric devilry. "Then"—when with wicked hands the creature had dared to crucify the Lord of Glory. He might have uttered awful maledictions over them. He might have let loose the thunderbolts of righteous wrath and slain them. He might have caused the earth to open her mouth so that they had gone down alive into the Pit. But no. Though subjected to unspeakable shame, though suffering excruciating pain, though despised, rejected, hated, nevertheless, He cries, "*Father, forgive them.*" That was the triumph of redeeming love. Love "suffereth long, and is kind . . . beareth all things . . . endureth all things" (1 Cor. 13:4, 7). Thus it was shown at the Cross.

When Samson came to his dying hour, he used his great strength of body to encompass the destruction of his foes; but the Perfect One exhibited the strength of His love by praying for the forgiveness of His enemies. Matchless grace! "Matchless," we say, for even Stephen failed to fully follow out the blessed example set by the Saviour. If the reader will turn to Acts 7, he will find that Stephen's first thought was of himself, and then he prayed for his enemies—"And they stoned Stephen, calling upon God, and saying, Lord Jesus, receive my spirit. And he kneeled down and cried with a loud voice, Lord, lay not this sin to their charge" (Acts 7:59–60). But with Christ the order was reversed: *He* prayed first for His foes, and last for Himself. In *all things* He has the preeminence.

And now one concluding word of application and exhortation. Should this chapter have been read by an unsaved person, we would earnestly ask him to weigh well the next sentence— How dreadful must it be to oppose Christ and His truth *knowingly*! Those who crucified the Saviour "knew not what they did." But, my reader, there is a very real and solemn sense in which this is *not* true of you. *You know* you ought to receive Christ as your Saviour, that you *ought* to crown Him the Lord of your life, that you *ought* to make it your first and last concern to please and glorify Him. Be warned then: your danger is great. If you deliberately turn from Him, you turn from the *only* One who can save you from your sins, and it is written, "If we sin wilfully after that we have received the knowledge of the truth, there remaineth no more sacrifice for sins, but a certain fearful looking for of judgment and of fiery indignation, which shall devour the adversaries" (Heb. 10:26–27).

It only remains for us to add a word on the blessed *completeness* of divine forgiveness. Many of God's people are unsettled and troubled upon this point. They understand that all the sins they had committed before they received Christ as their Saviour have been forgiven, but oftentimes they are not clear concerning the sins that they commit *after* they have been born again. Many suppose it is possible for them to sin away the pardon that God had bestowed upon them. They suppose that the blood of Christ dealt with their past only, and that so far as the present and the future are concerned, they have to take care of that themselves. But of what value would be a pardon that might be taken away from me at any time? Surely there can be no settled peace when my acceptance with God and *my* going to heaven is made to depend upon *my* holding on to Christ, or *my* obedience and faithfulness.

Blessed by God, the forgiveness that He bestows covers *all* sins—past, present, and future. Fellow believer, did not Christ bear our "*sins*" in His own body on the Tree? And were not *all your* sins *future* sins when He died? Surely, for at that time you had not been born, and so had not committed a single sin. Very well then: Christ bore your "future" sins as truly as your past ones. What the Word of God teaches is that the unbelieving soul is brought out of the place of unforgiveness into *the place* to which forgiveness attaches. Christians are a forgiven *people*. Says the Holy Spirit: "Blessed is the man to whom the Lord *will not* impute sin" (Rom. 4:8, emphasis added)! The believer is *in Christ*, and there sin will never again be imputed to us. This is our place or position before God. In Christ is where

31

He beholds us. And because I am in Christ, I am completely and eternally forgiven, so much so that never again will sin be laid to my charge as touching my salvation, even though I were to remain on earth a hundred years. I am out of that place forevermore. Listen to the testimony of Scripture: "And you being dead in your sins and the uncircumcision of your flesh, hath he [God] *quickened together with him [Christ],* having forgiven you *all* trespasses" (Col. 2:13, emphasis added). Mark the two things that are here united (and what God hath joined together let not man put asunder)—my union with a risen Christ is connected with my forgiveness! If, then, my life is "hid with Christ in God" (Col. 3:3), then I am forever out of the place where *imputation* of sin applies. Hence it is written, "There is therefore now *no condemnation* to them which are in Christ Jesus" (Rom. 8:1, emphasis added)—how could there be if "*all*" trespasses" have been forgiven? None can lay *anything* to the charge of God's elect (Rom. 8:33). Christian reader, join the writer in praising God because we are *eternally forgiven everything.**

---

*It should be added by way of explanation that it is the *judicial* aspect we have dealt with. *Restorative* forgiveness—which is the bringing back again into communion of a sinning believer—dealt with in 1 John 1:9—is another matter altogether.

2

The Word of Salvation

And he said unto Jesus, Lord, remember me when thou
comest into thy kingdom.
And Jesus said unto him, Verily I say unto thee, Today shalt
thou be with me in paradise.

Luke 23:42–43

The second of Christ's cross utterances was spoken in response
to the request of the dying thief. Ere considering the words of
the Saviour, we shall first ponder what occasioned them.

It was no accident that the Lord of Glory was crucified
between two thieves. There are no accidents in a world that
is governed by God. Much less could there have been any accident on that day of all days, or in connection with that event
of all events—a day and an event that lie at the very center of
the world's history. No, God was presiding over that scene.
From all eternity He had decreed when and where and how
and with whom His Son should die. Nothing was left to chance
or the caprice of man. All that God had decreed came to pass
exactly as He had ordained, and nothing happened save as

He had eternally purposed. Whatsoever man did was simply that which God's hand and counsel "determined before to be done" (Acts 4:28).

When Pilate gave orders that the Lord Jesus should be crucified between the two malefactors, all unknown to himself, he was but putting into execution the eternal decree of God and fulfilling His prophetic word. Seven hundred years before this Roman officer gave his command, God had declared through Isaiah that His Son should be "numbered with the transgressors" (Isa. 53:12). How utterly unlikely this appeared, that the Holy One of God should be numbered with the unholy; that the very One whose finger had inscribed on the tables of stone the Sinaitic Law should be assigned a place with the lawless; that the Son of God should be executed with criminals—this seemed utterly inconceiveable. Yet it actually came to pass. Not a singe word of God can fall to the ground. "For ever, O LORD, thy word is settled in heaven" (Ps. 119:89). Just as God had ordained, and just as He had announced, so it came to pass.

Why did God order it that His beloved Son should be crucified between two criminals? Certainly God had a reason—a good one, a manifold one, whether we can discern it or not. God never acts arbitrarily. He has a good purpose for everything He does, for all His works are ordered by infinite wisdom. In this particular instance, a number of answers suggest themselves to our inquiry. Was not our blessed Lord crucified with the two thieves to fully demonstrate *the unfathomable depths of shame into which He had descended?* At His birth He was surrounded by the beasts of the field, and now, at His death, He is numbered with the refuse of humanity. Again, was not the Saviour numbered with the transgressors to show us *the position He occupied as our substitute?* He had taken the place that was due us, and what was that but the place of shame, the place of transgressors, the place of criminals condemned to death! Again, was He not deliberately humiliated thus by Pilate to exhibit *man's estimate of the peerless One—"despised"* as well as rejected! Again, was He not crucified with the two

34

thieves, so that in those three crosses and the ones who hung upon them we might have a vivid and concrete representation of *the drama of salvation and man's response thereto*—the Saviour's redemption, the sinner repenting and believing, and the sinner reviling and rejecting?

Another important lesson that we may learn from the crucifixion of Christ between the two thieves, and the fact that one received Him and the other rejected Him, is that of *the sovereignty of God*. The two malefactors were crucified together. They were equally near to Christ. Both of them saw and heard all that transpired during those fateful six hours. Both were notoriously wicked, both were suffering acutely, both were dying, and both urgently needed forgiveness. Yet one of them died in his sins, died as he had lived—hardened and impenitent; while the other repented of his wickedness, believed in Christ, called on Him for mercy and went to paradise. How can this be accounted for except by the sovereignty of God! We see precisely the same thing going on today. Under exactly the same circumstances and conditions, one is melted and another remains unmoved. Under the same sermon, one man will listen with indifference, while another will have his eyes opened to see his need and his will moved to close with God's offer of mercy. To one the Gospel is revealed; to another it is "hidden." Why? All we can say is, "Even so Father, for so it seemed good in Thy sight." And yet God's sovereignty is never meant to destroy human responsibility. Both are plainly taught in the Bible, and it is our business to believe and preach both whether we can harmonize or understand them or not. In preaching both, we may seem to our hearers to *contradict* ourselves, but what matters that? Said the late C. H. Spurgeon, when preaching on 1 Timothy 2:3–4, "There stands the text, and I believe that it is my Father's wish that 'all men should be saved, and come to the knowledge of the truth.' But I know, also, that He does not will it, so that He will save any one of them, unless they believe in His Son; for He has told us over and over again that He will not. He will not save any man except he forsakes his sins, and turns to Him with full purpose of heart: that I also know. And I know, also, that He has a people whom He will save, whom by His eternal love He has chosen and whom by His eternal power He will deliver. *I do not know how that squares with this, that is another of the things I do not know.*" And said this prince of preachers, "I will just stand to what I ever shall and always have preached, and take God's Word as it stands, *whether I can reconcile it with another part of God's Word or not.*" We say again, God's sovereignty is never meant to destroy man's responsibility. We are to make diligent use of all the means that God has appointed for the salvation of souls. We are bidden to preach the Gospel to "every creature." Grace is free; the invitation is broad enough to take in "whosoever believeth." Christ turns away none who come to Him. Yet, after we have done all, after we have planted and watered, it is God who "giveth the increase," and this He does as best pleaseth His sovereign will.

In the salvation of the dying thief, we have a clear view of *victorious grace* such as is to be found nowhere else in the Bible. God is the God of all grace, and salvation is entirely by His grace. "By grace are ye saved" (Eph. 2:8), and it is "by grace" from beginning to end. Grace planned salvation, grace provided salvation, and grace so works on and in His elect as to overcome the hardness of their hearts, the obstinacy of their wills, and the enmity of their minds, and thus makes them willing to *receive* salvation. Grace begins, grace continues, and grace consummates our salvation.

Salvation by grace—sovereign, irresistible, free grace—is illustrated in the New Testament by example as well as by precept. Perhaps the two most striking cases of all are those of Saul of Tarsus and the dying robber. And the case of the latter is even more noteworthy than the former. In the case of Saul, who afterward became Paul the apostle to the Gentiles, there was an exemplary moral character to begin with. Writing years afterward of his condition before his conversion, the apostle declared that as touching the righteousness of the law he was "blameless" (Phil. 3:6). He was a "Pharisee of the Pharisees": punctillious in his habits, correct in his deportment. Morally, his character was flawless. *After* his conversion, his life was one of Gospel righteousness. Constrained by the love of Christ, he spent himself in preaching the Gospel to sinners and in laboring to build up the saints. Doubtless our readers will agree with us when we say that probably Paul came nearest to attaining the ideals of the Christian life and that he followed after his Master more closely than any other saint has since. But with the saved thief, it was far otherwise. He had no moral life before his conversion and no life of active service after it. Before his conversion he respected neither the law of God nor the law of man. After his conversion he died without having opportunity to engage in the service of Christ. I would emphasize this, because these are the two things that are regarded by so many as contributing factors to our salvation. It is supposed that we must first fit ourselves by developing a noble character *before* God will receive us as His sons; and that *after* He has received us, tentatively, we are merely placed on probation, and that unless we now bring forth a certain quality and quantity of good works, we shall "fall from grace and be lost." But the dying thief *had no good works* either before or after conversion. Hence we are shut up to the conclusion that if saved at all, he was certainly saved *by sovereign grace.*

The salvation of the dying thief also disposes of another prop that the legality of the carnal mind interposes to rob God of the glory due unto His grace. Instead of attributing the salvation of lost sinners to the matchless grace of God, many professing Christians seek to account for them by human influences, instrumentalities, and circumstances. Either the preacher, or providential and propitious circumstances, or the prayers of believers are looked to as the main cause. Let us not be misunderstood here. It is true that often God is pleased to use means in the conversion of sinners; that frequently He condescends to bless our prayers and efforts to point sinners to Christ; that many times He causes His providences to awaken and arouse the ungodly to a realization of their state. But God is not shut up to these things. He is not limited to human instrumentalities. His grace is all-powerful, and when He pleases, that grace is able to save in spite of the *lack* of human instrumentalities and in the face of *un*favorable circumstances. So it was in the case of the saved thief. Consider—

His conversion occurred at a time when to outward appearance Christ had lost all power to save either Himself or others. This thief had marched along with the Saviour through the streets of Jerusalem and had seen Him sink beneath the weight of the Cross! It is highly probable that as one who followed the occupation of a thief and robber, this was the first day he had ever set eyes on the Lord Jesus, and now that he did see Him, it was under every circumstance of weakness and disgrace. His enemies were triumphing over Him. His friends had mostly forsaken Him. Public opinion was unanimously against Him. His very crucifixion was regarded as utterly inconsistent with His Messiahship. His lowly condition was a stumbling block to the Jews from the very first, and the circumstances of His death must have intensified it, especially to one who had never seen Him except in this condition. Even those who had believed on Him were made to doubt by His crucifixion. There was not one in the crowd who stood there with outstretched finger and cried, "Behold the Lamb of God, which taketh away the sin of the world" (John 1:29). And yet, notwithstanding these obstacles and difficulties in the way of this faith, the thief apprehended the Saviourhood and Lordship of Christ. How can we possibly account for such faith and such spiritual understanding in one circumstanced as he was? How can we explain the fact that this dying thief took a suffering, bleeding, crucified man for his God! It cannot be accounted for apart from *divine* intervention and supernatural operation. His faith in Christ was a *miracle of grace*!

It is also to be remarked that the thief's conversion took place *before* the supernatural phenomena of that day. He cried, "Lord, remember me" *before* the hours of darkness, *before* the triumphant cry "It is finished," *before* the rending of the temple veil, *before* the quaking of the earth and the shivering of the rocks, *before* the centurion's confession "Truly this was the Son of God." God purposely set his conversion before these things so that His sovereign grace might be magnified and His sovereign power acknowledged. God designedly chose to save this thief under the most *un*favorble circumstances that no flesh should glory in His presence. God deliberately arranged this combination of *un*propitious conditions and surroundings to teach us that "Salvation is of the Lord," to teach us *not* to magnify human instrumentality above divine agency, to teach us that every genuine conversion is the direct product of the *supernatural* operation of the Holy Spirit.

We shall now consider together the thief himself, his various utterances, his request of the Saviour, and our Lord's response—"And he said unto Jesus, Lord, remember me when thou comest into thy kingdom. And Jesus said unto him, Verily I say unto thee, Today shalt thou be with me in paradise" (Luke 23:42–43).

1. Here we see a representative sinner.

We shall never get to the heart of this incident until we regard the conversion of this man as a representative case, and the thief himself as a representative character. There are those who have sought to show that the original character of the repenting thief was nobler and worthier than that of the other who repented not. But this is not only not true to the facts of the case, but it serves to efface the peculiar glory of his conversion and takes away from the wonderment of God's grace. It is of great importance to see that prior to the time when the one repented and believed, there was *no* essential difference between the two thieves. In nature, in history, in circumstances, they were one. The Holy Spirit has been careful to tell us that they *both* reviled the suffering Saviour: "The chief priests mocking him, with the scribes and elders, said, He saved others; himself he cannot save. If he be the King of

Israel, let him now come down from the cross, and we will believe him. He trusted in God; let him deliver him now, if he will have him: for he said, I am the Son of God. The *thieves* also, which were crucified with him, cast the same in his teeth" (Matt. 27:41–44, emphasis added).

Terrible indeed was the condition and action of this robber. On the very brink of eternity, he unites with the enemies of Christ in the awful sin of mocking Him. This was unparalleled turpitude. Think of it—a man in his dying hour deriding the suffering Saviour! O what a demonstration of human depravity and of the native enmity of the carnal mind against God! And reader, by nature there is *the same* depravity inhering within *you*, and unless a miracle of divine grace has been wrought upon you, there is *the same* enmity against God and His Christ present in *your* heart. You may not think so; you may not feel so; you may not believe so. But that does not alter the fact. The Word of Him who cannot lie declares, "The heart is deceitful above all things, *and desperately wicked*" (Jer. 17:9, emphasis added). That is a statement of *universal* application. It describes what *every* human heart is by natural birth. And again the same Scripture of Truth declares, "The carnal mind is *enmity against God*: for it is not subject to the law of God, neither indeed can be" (Rom. 8:7). This too diagnoses the state of every descendant of Adam. "*For there is no difference*: for all have sinned, and come short of the glory of God" (Rom. 3:22–23). Unspeakably solemn is this, yet it needs to be pressed. It is not until our desperate condition is realized that we discover our need of a divine Saviour. It is not until we are brought to see our *total* corruption and unsoundness that we shall hasten to the Great Physician. It is not until we find in this dying thief a portrayal of ourselves that we shall join in saying, "Lord, remember *me*."

We have to be abased before we can be exalted. We have to be stripped of the filthy rags of our self-righteousness before we are ready for the garments of salvation. We have to come to God as beggars, empty-handed, before we can receive the

40

gift of eternal life. We have to take the place of *lost* sinners before Him if we would be saved. Yes, we have to acknowledge ourselves as *thieves* before we can have a place in the family of God. "But," you say, "I am no thief! I acknowledge I am not all I ought to be. I am not perfect. In fact, I will go so far as to admit I am a sinner. But I cannot allow that this thief represents *my* state and condition." Ah, friend, your case is far worse than you suppose. You *are* a thief, and that of the worst type. *You have robbed God!* Suppose that a firm in the East appointed an agent to represent them in the West, and that every month they forwarded to him his salary. But suppose also at the end of the year his employers discovered that though the agent had been cashing the checks they sent him, nevertheless, he had *served another firm* all that time. Would not that agent be a thief? Yet this is precisely the situation and state of every sinner. He has been sent into this world by God, and God has endowed him with talents and the capacity to use and improve them. God has blessed him with health and strength; He has supplied his every need and provided innumerable opportunities to serve and glorify Him. But with what result? The very things God has given him have been *mis*appropriated. The sinner has *served another master*, even Satan. He dissipates his strength and wastes his time in the pleasures of sin. He has robbed God. Unsaved reader, in the sight of heaven, your condition is as desperate and your heart is as wicked as that of the thief. See in him a picture of yourself.

2. Here we see that man has to come to the end of himself before he can be saved.

Above we have contemplated this dying robber as a representative sinner, a sample specimen of what all men are by nature and practice—by nature at enmity against God and His Christ; by practice robbers of God, misusing what He has given us and failing to render what is due Him. We are now to see that this crucified robber was also a representative case in his conversion. And at this point we shall dwell simply upon his *helplessness*.

To see ourselves as lost sinners is not sufficient. To learn that we are corrupt and depraved by nature and sinful transgressors by practice is the first important lesson. The *next* is to learn that we are utterly undone and that we can do *nothing* whatever to help ourselves. To discover that our condition is so desperate that it is entirely *beyond* human repair is the second step toward salvation—looking at it from the human side. But if man is slow to learn that he is a lost sinner and unfit for the presence of a holy God, he is slower still to recognize that he can do nothing toward his salvation and is unable to work any improvement in himself so as to be fit for God. Yet it is not until we realize that we are "without strength" (Rom. 5:6), that we are "impotent" (John 5:3), that it is *not* by works of righteousness that we do but by His mercy God saves us (Titus 3:5), not until then shall we *despair* of ourselves and look *outside* of ourselves to the One who can save us.

The great Scripture type of sin is *leprosy*, and for leprosy, man can devise no cure. God alone can deal with this dreadful disease. So it is with sin. But as we have said, man is slow to learn his lesson. He is like the prodigal son, who when he had squandered his substance in the far country in riotous living and began to be "in want," instead of returning to the father straightaway, he "went and joined himself to a citizen of that country" (Luke 15:15) and went to the fields to feed swine; in other words, he *went to work*. Likewise the sinner who has been aroused to his need, instead of going at once to Christ, he tries to work himself into God's favor. But he will fare no better than the prodigal—the husks of the swine will be his only portion. Or again, like the woman bowed down with her infirmity for many long years. She tried many physicians before she sought the Great Physician: so the awakened sinner seeks relief and peace in first one thing and then another, until he completes the weary round of religious performances, and ends by being "nothing bettered, but rather [grows] worse"

(Mark 5:26). No, it is not until that woman had "spent *all* she had" that she sought Christ: and it is not until the sinner comes to *the end* of his own resources that he will betake himself to the Saviour.

Before any sinner can be saved, he must come to the place of realized weakness. This is what the conversion of the dying thief shows us. What could *he* do? He could not walk in the paths of righteousness, for there was a nail through either foot. He could not perform any good works, for there was a nail through either hand. He could not turn over a new leaf and live a better life, for he was dying. And, my reader, those hands of yours that are so ready for self-righteous acting, and those feet of yours that are so swift to run in the way of legal obedience, must be nailed to the Cross. The sinner has to be *cut off* from his own workings and be made willing to be saved by Christ. A realization of your sinful condition, of your lost condition, of your helpless condition, is nothing more or less than old-fashioned conviction of sin, and this is the *sole* prerequisite for coming to Christ for salvation, for Christ Jesus came into the world to save *sinners*.

3. Here we see the meaning of repentance and faith.

Repentance may be considered under various aspects. It includes in its meaning and scope a change of mind about sin, a sorrowing for sin, a forsaking of sin. Yet there is more in repentance than these. Really, repentance is the realization of our lost condition; it is the discovery of our ruin; it is the judging of ourselves; it is the owning of our lost estate. Repentance is not so much an intellectual process as it is the conscience active in the presence of God. And this is exactly what we find here in the case of the thief. First he says to his companion, "Dost not thou fear God, seeing thou art in the same condemnation?" (Luke 23:40). A short time before he had mingled his voice with those who were reviling the Saviour. But the Holy Spirit had been at work upon him, and now his conscience is active in the presence of God. It was not, "Dost not thou fear *punishment*?"

but, "Dost not thou fear *God*?" He apprehends God as judge. And then, in the second place he adds, "And we indeed justly; for we receive *the due reward* of our deeds" (Luke 23:41). Here we see him acknowledging his guilt and the justice of his condemnation. He passes sentence upon himself. He makes no excuses and attempts no extenuation. He recognized he was a transgressor, and that, as such, he fully deserved punishment for his sins, yea, that death was his due. Have *you* taken this position before God, my reader? Have you openly confessed your sins to Him? Have you passed judgment upon yourself and your ways? Are you ready to acknowledge that *death* is your "due"? Whilever you palliate sin or prevaricate about it, you are shutting yourself out from Christ. Christ came into the world to save sinners—self-confessed sinners, sinners who really take *the place of sinners* before God, sinners who are conscious that they are *lost* and undone.

The thief's "repentance toward God" was accompanied with "faith toward our Lord Jesus Christ." In contemplating his faith, we may notice first that it was an *intelligent head faith*. In the earlier paragraphs of this chapter, we have called attention to the sovereignty of God and His irresistible and victorious grace, which were exhibited in the conversion of this thief. Now we turn to the other side of the truth, equally necessary to press, a side that is not contradictory to what we have said previously but rather complementary and supplementary. Scripture does not teach that if God has elected a certain soul to be saved, that that person *will be saved* whether they believe or not. That is a false conclusion drawn by those who reject the truth. No, Scripture teaches that the same God who predestined the end also predestined the means. The God who decreed the salvation of the dying thief *fulfilled* His decree by giving him a faith with which to believe. This is the plain teaching of 2 Thessalonians 2:13 and other Scriptures—"God hath from the beginning chosen you to salvation through sanctification of the Spirit and belief of the truth." This is just what we see here in connection with this robber. He "believed the truth."

His faith took hold of the Word of God. Over the Cross was the superscription, "This is Jesus the King of the Jews." Pilate had placed it there in derision. But it was the truth nevertheless, and after he had written it, God would not allow him to alter it. The board bearing this superscription had been carried in front of Christ through the streets of Jerusalem and out to the place of crucifixion, and the thief had read it, and divine grace and power had opened the eyes of his understanding to see it *was* the truth. His faith grasped the Kingship of Christ, hence his mention of "when thou comest *into thy kingdom.*" Faith always rests on the written Word of God.

Before a man will believe that Jesus is the Christ, he must have the testimony before him that Jesus *is* the Christ. Distinction is often made between head faith and heart faith, and properly so, for the distinction is real and vital. Sometimes head faith is decribed as valueless, but this is foolish. There must be head faith before there can be heart faith. We must believe *intellectually* before we can believe *savingly* in the Lord Jesus. Proof of this is seen in connection with the heathen: they have no head faith, and therefore they have no heart faith. We readily grant that head faith will not save *unless* it be accompanied by heart faith, but we insist that there is no heart faith unless there has first been head faith. How can they believe *in* Him *of* whom they have not heard? True, one may believe *about* Him without believing *in* Him, but one cannot believe in Him without first believing about Him. So it was with the dying thief. In all probability he had never seen Christ before this day of his death, but he had seen the written superscription testifying to His Kingship, and the Holy Spirit used this as the basis of his faith. We say, then, that his was an intelligent faith: first an intellectual faith, the believing of the written testimony submitted to him; second, a heart faith, the resting in confidence on Christ Himself as the Saviour of sinners.

Yes, this dying robber exercised *a heart faith that rested savingly on Christ.* We shall try to be very simple here. A man may have head faith in the Lord Jesus and be lost. A man may

45

believe about the historic Christ and be no better for it, just as he is no better for believing about the historic Napoleon. Reader, you may believe all *about* the Saviour—His perfect life, His sacrificial death, His victorious resurrection, His glorious ascension, His promised return—but you must do more than this. Gospel faith is a *confiding* faith. Saving faith is more than a correct opinion or a train of reasoning. Saving faith *transcends* all reason. Look at this dying thief! Was it reasonable that Christ should notice him?—a crucified robber, a self-confessed criminal, one who a few mintues ago had been *reviling* Him! Was it reasonable that the Saviour should take any notice of him? Was it *reasonable* to expect that *he* should be transported from the very brink of the Pit into paradise? Ah, my reader, the head reasons, but *the heart* does not. And this man's petition came from his heart. He had not the use of his hands and feet (and they are not needed for salvation; they rather impede), but he *had* the use of his heart and tongue. They were free to believe and confess—"with the heart man believeth unto righteousness; and with the mouth confession is made unto salvation" (Rom. 10:10).

We may also notice his was a *humble* faith. He prayed with becoming modesty. It was not "Lord, honor me," or "Lord, exalt me," but "Lord, if thou wilt but think of me! if thou wilt only look on me"—"Lord, *remember* me." And yet that word "remember" was wonderfully *full and appropriate*. He might have said, "Pardon me, save me, bless me"; but "remember" included them all. An interest in *Christ's heart* will include an interest in all His benefits! Moreover, this word was well suited to the *condition* of the one who uttered it. He was an outcast from society—who would *remember* him! The public would think no more of him. His friends would be glad to forget him as having disgraced his family. But there is One with whom he ventures to lodge this petition—*"Lord, remember me."*

Finally, we may notice that his was a *courageous* faith. Perhaps this is not apparent at first sight, but a little consideration will make it plain. He who hung on the central cross was the one on whom all eyes were turned and toward whom all the the vile mockery of a vulgar mob was directed. Every faction of that crowd joined in jeering at the Saviour. Matthew tells us that "they that passed by reviled him," that "likewise also the chief priests [mocked] him, with the scribes and elders." While Luke informs us "the soldiers also mocked him" (23:36). It is therefore easy to understand why the thieves should also take up the taunting cry. No doubt the priests and scribes smiled benignly upon them as they did so. But suddenly there was a change. The repenting thief instead of continuing to sneer and jibe at Christ turns to his companion and openly rebukes him in the hearing of the spectators gathered around the crosses, crying, "This man hath done nothing amiss" (Luke 23:41). Thus he *condemned* the whole Jewish nation! But more; not only does he bear testimony to Christ's innocency, but he also confessed His Kingship. And thus by a single stroke he cuts himself off from *the favor* of his companion and of the crowd as well! We talk today of the courage that is needed to openly witness for Christ, but such courage in these days pales into utter insignificance before the courage displayed that day by the dying thief.

4. Here we see a marvelous case of spiritual illumination.

It is perfectly wonderful the progress made by this man in those few dying hours. His growth in grace and in the knowledge of his Lord was amazing. From the brief record of the words that fell from his lips, we may discover *seven* things that he had learned under the tuition of the Holy Spirit.

First, he expresses *his belief in a future life* where *retribution* would be meted out by a righteous and sin-avenging God. "Dost not thou fear God?" proves this. He sharply reprimands his companion, and as much as says, How dare you have the temerity to revile this innocent man? Remember that shortly you will have to appear before God and face a tribunal infinitely more solemn than the one that sentenced you to be crucified. God is to be *feared*, so be silent.

Second, as we have seen, *he had a sight of his own sinful- ness*—"thou art in the same condemnation? And we indeed justly; for we receive the due reward of our deeds" (Luke 23:40–41). He recognized that he was a transgressor. He saw that sin merited punishment, that "condemnation" was just. He owned that death was his "due." This was something that his companion neither confessed nor recognized.

Third, *he bore testimony to Christ's sinlessness*—"This man hath done nothing amiss" (Luke 23:41). And here we may mark the pains God took to guard the spotless character of His Son. Especially is this to be seen toward the end. Judas was moved to say, "I have betrayed *innocent* blood." Pilate testified, "I find *no fault* in him." Pilate's wife said, "Have nothing to do with this *just* man." And now that He hangs on the Cross, God opens the eyes of this robber to see the faultlessness of His beloved Son, and opens his lips so that he bears witness to His excellency.

Fourth, he not only witnessed to the sinless humanity of Christ, but *he also confessed His Godhead*—"*Lord*, remember me," he said. A marvelous word was that. The Saviour nailed to the Tree, the object of Jewish hatred and the butt of a vulgar mob's ridicule. This thief had heard the scornful challenge of the priests. "If thou be the Son of God, come down from the cross," and no response had been given. But moved by faith and not by sight, he recognizes and owns the Deity of the central sufferer.

Fifth, *he believed in the Saviourhood of the Lord Jesus*. He had heard Christ's prayer for His enemies, "Father, forgive them," and to one whose heart the Lord had opened, that short sentence became a saving sermon. His own cry, "Lord, remember me" included within its scope, "Lord, *save* me," which therefore implies his faith in the Lord Jesus as Saviour. In fact, he must have believed that Jesus was a Saviour for the *chief* of sinners, or how could he have believed that Christ would "remember" such as he!

Sixth, *he evidenced his faith in Christ's Kingship*—"when thou comest *into thy kingdom.*" This too was a wonderful word. Outward circumstances all seemed to belie His Kingship. Instead of being seated on a throne, He hung upon a cross. Instead of wearing a royal diadem, His brow was encircled with thorns. Instead of being waited upon by a retinue of servants, He was numbered with transgressors. Nevertheless, He *was* King—King of the Jews (Matt. 2:2).

Finally, *he looked forward to the second coming of Christ*—"*when thou comest.*" He looked away from the present to the future. He saw beyond the "sufferings" to the "glory." Over the cross, the eye of faith detected the crown. And in this he was before the apostles, for unbelief had closed their eyes. Yes, he looked beyond the first advent in shame to the second advent in power and majesty.

And how can we account for the spiritual intelligence of this dying robber? When did he receive such insight into the things of Christ? How comes it that this babe in Christ made such amazing progress in the school of God? It can be accounted for *only* by divine influence. The Holy Spirit was his teacher! Flesh and blood had not revealed these things unto him but the Father in heaven. What an illustration that divine things are hidden from "the wise and prudent" and are revealed to "babes"!

5. Here we see the Saviourhood of Christ.

The crosses were only a few feet apart, and it did not take the Saviour long to hear this cry of the penitent thief. What was His response thereto? He might have said, You deserve your fate: you are a wicked robber and have merited death. Or He might have replied, You have left it till too late: you should have sought Me sooner. Ah! but had He not promised, "Him that cometh to me I will in no wise cast out!" So it proved here.

Of the reproaches that were cast on Him by the crowd, the Lord Jesus took no notice. To the insulting challenge of the priests to descend from the Cross, He made no response. But the prayer of this contrite, believing thief arrested His attention. At the time He was grappling with the powers of darkness and sustaining the awful load of His people's guilt, and we should have thought He might be excused from attending to individual applications. Ah! but a sinner can never come to Christ in an *un*acceptable time. He gives him an answer of peace and that without delay.

The salvation of the repentant and believing robber illustrates not only Christ's *readiness* but also His *power* to save sinners. The Lord Jesus is no feeble Saviour. Blessed be God; He is able to "save unto the uttermost" them that come unto God by Him. And never was this so signally displayed as when on the Cross. This was the time of the Redeemer's "weakness" (2 Cor. 13:4). When the thief cried "Lord, remember me," the Saviour was in agony on the accursed Tree. Yet even then, even there, He had power to redeem this soul from death and open for him the gates of paradise! Never doubt, then, or question the infinite sufficiency of the Saviour. If a dying Saviour could save, how much more He who rose in triumph from the tomb, never more to die! In saving this thief, Christ gave an exhibition of His power at the very time when it was almost clouded.

The salvation of the dying thief demonstrates that the Lord is willing and able to save *all who come to Him.* If Christ received this penitent, believing thief, then none need despair of a welcome if they will but come to Christ. If this dying robber was *not beyond* the reach of divine mercy, then none are who will respond to the invitations of divine grace. The Son of Man came "to seek and to save that which was lost" (Luke 19:10), and none can sink lower than that. The Gospel of Christ is the power of God "to *every one* that believeth" (Rom. 1:16). O limit not the grace of God. A Saviour is provided for the very *chief* of sinners (1 Tim. 1:15), if only he will believe. Even those who reach the dying hour yet in their sins are not beyond hope. Personally I believe that very, very few are saved on a deathbed, and it is the height of folly for any man to postpone his salvation till then, for there is no guarantee that any man will have a death*bed*. Many are cut off suddenly, without any opportunity to lie down and die. Yet even one on a deathbed is not *beyond* the reach of divine mercy. As said one of the Puritans, "There is one such case recorded that none need despair, but *only one*, in Scripture, that none might presume."

Yes, here we see the Saviourhood of Christ. He came into this world to save sinners, and He left it and went to paradise accompanied by a saved criminal—the first trophy of His redeeming blood!

6. Here we see the destination of the saved at death.

In his splendid book *The Seven Sayings of Christ on the Cross*, Dr. Anderson-Berry has pointed out that the word "today" is not correctly placed in the rendering of our King James Version, and that the designed correspondence between the thief's request and Christ's response requires a different construction of the latter. The *form* of Christ's reply is evidently designed to *match* in its *order* of thought the robber's petition. This will be seen if we arrange the two in parallel couplets thus:

> And he said unto Jesus
> And Jesus said unto him
> Lord
> Verily I say unto thee
> Remember me
> Shalt thou be with me
> When thou comest
> Today
> Into thy kingdom
> In paradise.

By arranging the words thus, we discover the correct emphasis. "Today" is the emphatic word. In our Lord's gracious response to the thief's request, we have a striking illustration of how divine grace *exceeds* human expectations. The thief prayed that the Lord would remember him in His coming kingdom, but Christ assures him that before that very day had passed he should be with the Saviour. The thief asked to be remembered in an earthly kingdom, but Christ assured him of a place in paradise. The thief simply asked to be "remembered," but the Saviour declared he should be "with him." Thus doeth God exceeding abundantly *above* all that we ask or think.

Not only does Christ's reply signify the survival of the soul after the death of the body, but it tells us that the believer is *with Him* during the interval that divides death from the resurrection. To make this the more emphatic, Christ prefaced His promise with the solemn but assuring words "*Verily* I say unto you." It was this prospect of going to Christ at death that cheered the martyr Stephen in his last hour, and therefore did he cry, "*Lord Jesus*, receive my spirit" (Acts 7:59, emphasis added). It was this blessed expectation that moved the apostle Paul to say, I have "a desire to depart, and to be *with Christ*; which is far better" (Phil. 1:23, emphasis added). Not unconsciousness in the grave but with Christ *in paradise* is what awaits every believer at death. Every "believer" I say, for the souls of unbelievers, instead of going to paradise, pass to the place of torments, as is clear from our Lord's teaching in Luke 16. Reader, whither would *your* soul go, if this moment you were dying?

How hard Satan has striven to hide this blessed prospect from the saints of God! On the one hand, he has propagated the doleful dogma of soul sleep, the teaching that believers are in a state of unconsciousness between death and the resurrection; and on the other hand, he has invented a horrible purgatory, to terrify believers with the thought that at death they pass into fire, necessary to purify and fit them for heaven. How thoroughly the word of Christ to the thief disposes of these God-dishonoring delusions! The thief went straight from the cross to paradise! The moment a sinner believes, that moment is he "made meet to be a partaker of the inheritance of the saints in light" (Col. 1:12). "For by one offering he hath perfected for ever them that are sanctified" (Heb. 10:14). Our *fitness* for Christ's presence, as well as our *title*, rests solely on His shed blood.

7. Here we see the longing of the Saviour for fellowship.

In fellowship we reach the climax of grace and the sum of Christian privilege. Higher than fellowship we cannot go. God has called us "unto the fellowship of his Son" (1 Cor. 1:9). We are often told that we are "saved to serve," and this is true, but it is only a part of the truth and by no means the most wondrous and blessed part of it. We are saved for fellowship. God had innumerable "servants" *before* Christ came here to die—the *angels* ever do His bidding. Christ came not primarily to secure servants but those who should enter into fellowship with Himself.

That which makes heaven superlatively attractive to the heart of the saint is not that heaven is a place where we shall be delivered from all sorrow and suffering, nor is it that heaven is the place where we shall meet again those we loved in the Lord, nor is it that heaven is the place of golden streets and pearly gates and jasper walls—no; blessed as these things are, *heaven without Christ would not be heaven.* It is Christ the heart of the believer longs for and pants after—"Whom have I in heaven but thee? and there is none upon earth that I desire beside thee" (Ps. 73:25). And the most amazing thing is that heaven will not be heaven to Christ in the highest sense until His redeemed are gathered around Him. It is His saints that His heart longs for. To come again and "receive us *unto himself*" is the joyous expectation set before Him. Not until He sees of the travail of His soul will He be fully *satisfied.*

These are the thoughts suggested and confirmed by the words of the Lord Jesus to the dying thief. "Lord, remember me" had been his cry. And what was the response? Note it carefully. Had Christ merely said, "Verily I say unto thee, Today thou shalt be in paradise," that would have set at rest the fears of the thief. Yes, but it did not satisfy the Saviour. That upon which His heart was set was the fact that that very day a soul saved by His precious blood should be *with Him* in paradise! We say again, this is the climax of grace and the sum of Christian blessing. Said the apostle, "I have a desire to depart, and to *be with Christ*" (Phil. 1:23, emphasis added). And again, he wrote, "Absent from the body"—free from all pain and care? No. "Absent from the body"—translated to glory? No. "Absent from the body . . . *present with the Lord*" (2 Cor. 5:8, emphasis added). So too with Christ. Said He, "In my Father's house are many mansions: if it were not so, I would have told you. I go to prepare a place for you"; yet when He adds, "I will come again," He does not say "And conduct you unto the Father's house," or "I will take you to the place I have prepared for you," but "I will come again, *and receive you unto myself*" (John 14:2–3, emphasis added). To "be ever with the Lord" (1 Thess. 4:17) is the goal of all *our* hopes; to have us forever with Himself is that to which *He* looks forward with eager and gladsome expectation. Thou shalt be *with Me* in paradise!

3

The Word of Affection

Now there stood by the cross of Jesus his mother. . . .
When Jesus therefore saw his mother,
and the disciple standing by, whom he loved
he saith unto his mother,
Woman, behold thy son!
Then saith he to the disciple,
Behold thy mother!

John 19:25–27

"Now there stood by the cross of Jesus his mother" (John 19:25). Like her son, Mary was not unacquainted with grief. At the beginning we are told, "And the angel came in unto her, and said, Hail, thou that art highly favoured, the Lord is with thee: blessed art thou among women. And when she saw him, she was *troubled* at his saying, and cast in her mind what manner of salutation this should be" (Luke 1:28–29). This was but the forerunner of many troubles: Gabriel had come to announce to her the fact of the miraculous conception, and a moment's reflection will show us that it was no light matter for Mary to become the mother of our Lord in this mysterious and unheard of way. It brought with it, no doubt, at a distant date, great honor, but it brought with it for the present no small danger to Mary's reputation, and no small trial to her faith. It is beautiful to observe her quiet submission to the will of God—"And Mary said, Behold the handmaid of the Lord; *be it unto me according to thy word*" (Luke 1:38, emphasis added), was her response. This was lovely resignation. Nevertheless, she was "troubled" at the Annunciation, and as we have said, this was but the precursor of many trials and sorrows.

What sorrow it must have caused her when, because there was no room in the inn, she had to lay her newly born babe in the manger! What anguish must have been hers when she learned of Herod's purpose to destroy her infant's life! What trouble was given her when she was forced on His account to flee into a foreign country and sojourn for several years in the land of Egypt! What piercings of soul must have been hers when she saw her son despised and rejected of men! What grief must have wrung her heart as she beheld Him hated and persecuted by His own nation! And who can estimate what she passed through as she stood there at the Cross? If Christ was the Man of Sorrows, was she not the woman of sorrows?

"There stood by the cross of Jesus his mother" (John 19:25).

1. Here we see the fulfillment of Simeon's prophecy.

In accordance with the requirements of the Mosaic law, the parents of the child Jesus brought Him to the temple to present Him to the Lord. Then it was that old Simeon, who waited for the consolation of Israel, took Him into his arms and blessed God. After saying, "Lord, now lettest thy servant depart in peace, according to thy word: for mine eyes have seen thy salvation, which thou hast prepared before the face of all people; a light to lighten the Gentiles, and the glory of thy people Israel" (Luke 2:29–32)—he now turned to Mary and said, "Behold, this child is set for the fall and rising again of many in Israel; and for a sign which shall be spoken against; (yea, *a sword shall pierce through thy own soul also,*) *that* the thoughts of many hearts may be revealed" (Luke 2:34–35, emphasis added). A strange word was that! Could it be that hers, the greatest of all privileges, was to bring with it the greatest of all sorrows? It seemed most unlikely at the time Simeon spoke. Yet how truly and how tragically did it come to pass! Here at the Cross was this prophecy of Simeon fulfilled.

"Now there stood by the cross of Jesus his mother" (John 19:25). After the days of His infancy and childhood, and during all the public ministry of Christ, we see and hear so little of Mary. Her life was lived in the background, among the shadows. But now, when the supreme hour strikes of her Son's agony, when the world has cast out the child of her womb, she stands there by the Cross! Who can fitly portray such a picture? Mary was nearest to the cruel Tree! Bereft of faith and hope, baffled and paralyzed by the strange scene, yet bound with the golden chain of love to the dying One, there she stands! Try and read the thoughts and emotions of that mother's heart. O what a sword it was that pierced her soul then! Never such bliss at a human birth, never such sorrow at an inhuman death.

Here we see displayed *the mother heart. She* is the dying man's mother. The One who agonizes there on the Cross is *her* child. She it was who first planted kisses on that brow now crowned with thorns. She it was who guided those hands and feet in their first infantile movements. No mother ever suffered as she did. His disciples may desert Him, His friends may forsake Him, His nation may despise Him, but His mother stands there at the foot of His cross. O who can fathom or analyze the mother heart.

Who can measure those hours of sorrow and suffering as the sword was slowly drawn through Mary's soul! Hers was no hysterical or demonstrative sorrow. There was no show of feminine weakness, no wild outcry of uncontrollable anguish, no fainting. Not a word that fell from her lips has been recorded by either of the four evangelists: apparently she suffered in unbroken silence. Yet her sorrow was nonetheless real and acute. Still waters run deep. She saw that brow pierced with cruel thorns, but she could not smooth it with her tender touch. She watched His pierced hands and feet grow numb and livid, but she might not chafe them. She marks His need of a drink, but she is not allowed to slake His thirst. She suffered in profound desolation of spirit.

"There *stood* by the cross of Jesus his mother" (John 19:25). The crowds are mocking, the thieves are taunting, the priests are jeering, the soldiers are callous and indifferent, the Saviour is bleeding, dying—and there is His mother beholding the horrible mockery. What wonder if she had swooned at such a sight! What wonder if she had turned away from such a spectacle! What wonder if she had fled from such a scene. But no! There she is: she does not crouch away, she does not faint, she does not even sink to the ground in her grief—she *stands*. Her action and attitude are unique. In all the annals of the history of our race, there is no parallel. What transcendent courage. She stood by the Cross of Jesus—what marvelous fortitude. She represses her grief and stands there silent. Was it not *reverence* for the Lord that kept her from disturbing His last moments?

> When Jesus therefore saw his mother, and the disciple standing by, whom he loved, he saith unto his mother, Woman, behold thy son! Then saith he to the disciple, Behold thy mother! And from that hour that disciple *took her unto his own home*.
>
> John 19:26–27, emphasis added

2. Here we see the perfect man setting an example for children to honor their parents.

The Lord Jesus evidenced His perfection in the manner in which He fully discharged the obligations of every relationship that He sustained, either to God or to man. On the Cross we behold His tender care and solicitude for His mother, and in this we have the pattern of Jesus Christ presented to all children for their imitation, teaching them how to acquit themselves toward their parents according to the laws of nature and grace.

The words that the finger of God engraved on the two tablets of stone, which were given to Moses on Mount Sinai, have never been repealed. They are in force while the earth lasts. Each of them is embodied in the perceptive teaching of the New Testament. The words of Exodus 20:12 are reiterated in Ephesians 6:1–3—"Children, obey your parents in the Lord: for this is right. Honour thy father and mother; which is the first commandment with promise; that it may be well with thee, and thou mayest live long on the earth."

The commandment for children to *honor* their parents goes far beyond a bare obedience to this expressed will, though, of course, it includes that. It embraces love and affection, gratitude and respect. It is too often assumed that this fifth commandment is addressed to young folks only. Nothing can be further from the truth. Unquestionably it is addressed to children first, for in the order of nature, children are always young first. But the conclusion that this commandment loses force when childhood is left behind is to miss at least half of its deep significance. As intimated, the word "honor" looks beyond obedience, though that is its first import. In the course of time, the children grow to manhood and womanhood, which is the age of full personal responsibility, the age when they are no longer beneath the control of their parents, yet has not their *obligations* to them ceased. They owe their parents a debt that they can never fully discharge. The very least they can do is to hold their parents in high esteem, to put them in the place of superiority, to reverence them. In the perfect exemplar we find both obedience and esteem manifested.

The fact that the last Adam came into this world not as did the first Adam—in full possession of the distinguishing glories of humanity: fully developed in body and mind—but as a babe, having to pass through the period of childhood, is a fact of tremendous importance and value in the light it casts on the fifth commandment. During His early years, the boy Jesus was under the control of Mary, His mother, and Joseph, His legal father. This is beautifully displayed in the second chapter of Luke. Arrived at the age of twelve, Jesus is taken by them to Jerusalem at the feast of the Passover. The picture presented is deeply suggestive if due attention is paid to it. At the close of the feast, Joseph and Mary depart for Nazareth, accompanied by their friends and supposing that Jesus is with them. But, instead, He had remained behind in the royal city. After a day's journey His absence is discovered. At once they turn back to Jerusalem, and there they find Him in the temple. His mother interrogates Him thus: "Son, why hast thou thus dealt with us? Behold, thy father and I have sought thee sorrowing" (Luke 2:48). The fact she had sought Him "sorrowing" strongly implies that He had hardly ever been outside the immediate sphere of her influence. Not to find Him at hand was to her a new and strange experience, and the fact that she, assisted by Joseph, had sought Him "sorrowing" reveals the beautiful relationship existing between them in the home at Nazareth! The answer that Jesus returned to her inquiry, when rightly understood, also reveals the honor in which He held His mother. We quite agree with Dr. Campbell Morgan that Christ does not here *rebuke* her. It is largely a matter of finding the right emphasis—"Wist *ye* not?" As the aforementioned expositor well says, "It was as though He had said: 'Mother, surely *you* knew Me well enough to know that nothing could detain Me but the affairs of the Father.'" The sequel is equally beautiful, for we read, "And he went down with them, and came to Nazareth, *and was subject unto them*" (Luke 2:51). And thus for all time the Christ of God has set the example for children to obey their parents.

But more. As it is with us, so it was with Christ: the years of obedience to Mary and Joseph ended, but not so the years of "honor." In the last and awful hours of His human life, amid the infinite sufferings of the Cross, the Lord Jesus thought of her who loved Him and whom He loved; thought of her present necessity and provided for her future need by committing her to the care of that disciple who most deeply understood His love. His thought for Mary at that time and the honor He gave her was one of the manifestations of His victory over pain.

Perhaps a word is called for in connection with our Lord's form of address—"Woman." So far as the record of the four Gospels go, never once did He call her "Mother." For us who live today, the reason for this is not hard to discern. Looking down the centuries with His omniscient foresight and seeing the awful system of Mariolatry so soon to be erected, He refrained from using a word that would in any wise countenance this idolatry—the idolatry of rendering to Mary the homage that is due alone her son: the idolatry of worshipping her as "The Mother of God."

Twice over in the Gospel records do we find our Lord addressing Mary as "Woman," and it is most noteworthy that *both* of these are found in *John's* Gospel, which, as is well known, set forth our Saviour's Deity. The synoptists set Him forth in *human* relationships; not so the fourth Gospel. John's Gospel presents Christ as the Son of God, and as *Son of God*, He is above all human relationships, and hence the perfect consonance of presenting the Lord Jesus *here* addressing Mary as "Woman."

Our Lord's act on the Cross in commending Mary to the care of His beloved apostle is better understood in the light of His mother's *widowhood.* Though the Gospels do not specifically record his death, there is little doubt but that Joseph died sometime before the Lord Jesus began His public ministry. Nothing is seen of Mary's husband after the incident recorded in Luke 2 when Christ was a boy of twelve. In John 2 Mary is seen at the Cana marriage, but no hint is given that Joseph was present. It was in view, then, of Mary's *widowhood*, in view of the fact that the time had now arrived when Jesus might no longer be a comfort to her by His bodily presence, that His loving care is manifested.

Permit just a brief word of exhortation. Probably these lines may be read by numbers of grown-up people who still have living fathers and mothers. How are you treating them? Are you truly "honoring" them? Does this example of Christ on the Cross put you to shame? It may be you are young and vigorous, and your parents gray headed and infirm; but saith the Holy Spirit, "Despise not thy mother when she is old" (Prov. 23:22). It may be you are rich, and they are poor; then fail not to make provision for them. It may be they live in a distant state or land, then neglect not to write them words of appreciation and cheer, which shall brighten their closing days. These are sacred *duties.* "Honour *thy* father *and* mother."

3. Here we see that John had returned to the Saviour's side.

Excepting, of course, the suffering of Christ at the hand of God, perhaps the bitterest dreg of all in the cup that He drank was the forsaking of Him by the apostles. It was bad enough and sad enough that His own people, the Jews, should despise and reject Him; but it was far worse that the eleven, who had companied so long with Him, should desert their Lord in the hour of crisis. One would have thought that *their* faith and *their* love was equal to any shock. But it was not. They *all* "forsook him, and fled" (Matt. 26:56) reads the sacred narrative. Unspeakably tragic was this. Their failure to "watch" with Him for one hour in the garden well nigh paralyzes our minds, but their turning away from Him at the time of His arrest almost baffles comprehension. Almost, we say, for have we not learned from bitter experience the deceitfulness of *our* hearts, how feeble *our* faith is, how lamentably weak *we* are in the hour of trial and testing! But for the grace of God, the veriest trifle is sufficient to overturn us. Let the restraining and upholding power of God be withdrawn from us, and how long would *we* stand?

The Lord Jesus had solemnly warned these disciples of their approaching cowardice—"Then saith Jesus unto them, All ye shall be offended because of me this night: for it is written, I will smite the shepherd, and the sheep of the flock shall be scattered abroad" (Matt. 26:31). And not Peter only but all of the apostles affirmed their determination to stand by Him—"Peter said unto him, Though I should die with thee, yet will I not deny thee. Likewise also said all the disciples" (Matt. 26:35). Nevertheless, *His* word proved true, and they all basely deserted Him. And how this reflected upon His glory! By their sinful flight, they exposed the Lord Jesus to the contempt and scoffs of His enemies. It was because of this we read, "The high priest then asked Jesus *of his disciples*" (John 18:19, emphasis added). It is not difficult to fill in the blanks. Doubtless Caiaphas inquired how many disciples He had, and what was become of them now? And what was the reason they had forsaken their master and left Him to shift for Himself when danger appeared? But observe that to this question the Saviour made no reply. *He* would not accuse them to the common enemy though they had deserted Him!

They forsook Him because they were "offended" at Him—"All ye shall be offended because of me this night" (Matt. 26:31): the Greek word here translated offended might well be rendered "scandalized." They were ashamed to be found in His company. They deemed it no longer safe to remain with Him. As He gave Himself up, they considered it advisable to provide as well as they might for themselves and somewhere or other take refuge from the present storm that had overtaken Him. This from the human side.

From the divine side, their forsaking of Christ was due to the suspension of God's preserving and upholding grace. They were not accustomed to forsake Him. They never did so afterward. They would not have done so now had there been influences of power, zeal, and love from heaven upon them. But, then, how could Christ have borne the burden and heat of the day? How should He have trod the winepress alone? How should His sorrows have been unmitigated if they had adhered faithfully to Him? No, no, it must not be. Christ must not have the least relief or comfort from any creature, and therefore that He might be left alone to grapple with the wrath of God and man, the Lord for a time withholds His strengthening influences from them; and then like Samson when he was shorn of his locks, they were as weak as other men. "Be strong in the Lord, and in the power of his might" says the apostles—if that be withheld, our purposes and resolutions melt away before temptation like snow before the sun.

Yet mark that the cowardice and infidelity of the apostles was only temporary. Later, they *sought* Him at the appointed place in Galilee (Matt. 28:16). But is it not cheering to know that one of the eleven *did* seek Him out *before* He rose in triumph from the tomb? Yea, sought Him while He yet hung on the Cross of shame! And who might it be supposed this one was? Which of the little band of apostles shall demonstrate the superiority of *His* love? Even if the sacred narrative had concealed his identity, it would not have been a difficult task to supply his name. The fact that the Scripture we are now considering shows us *John* at the foot of the Cross is one of the silent yet sufficient witnesses to the divine inspiration of the Bible. It is one of those undesigned *harmonies* of the Word that attests the superhuman origin of the Scriptures. There is no hint that any other of the eleven were around the Cross, but the thoughtful reader would *expect* to find there "the disciple whom Jesus loved." And there he was. John *had* returned to the Saviour's side, and there receives from Him a blessed commission. How artless and how perfect are the silent harmonies of Scripture!

And now, once more, a brief word of exhortation. Is there one who reads these lines that has wandered away from the side of the Saviour, who is no longer enjoying sweet communion with Him, who is, in a word, a *backslider*! Perhaps in the hour of trial you denied Him. Perhaps in the time of testing you failed. You have given more thought to your own interests than to His. The honor of *His* name, which *you* bear, has been lost sight of. O may the arrow of conviction now enter your conscience. May divine grace melt your heart. May the power of God draw you back to Christ, where alone your soul can find satisfaction and peace. Here is *encouragement* for you. Christ did not *rebuke* John on returning; instead, His wondrous grace bestowed on him an unspeakable privilege. Cease, then, your wanderings and return at once to Christ, and He will greet you with a word of welcome and cheer; and who knows but what He has some honorous commission awaiting you!

4. Here we discover an illustration of Christ's prudence.

We have already seen how the act of Christ in committing Mary into the hands of His disciple was an expression of His tender love and foresight. For John to take charge of the widowed mother of the Saviour was a blessed commission, and albeit, a precious legacy. When Christ said to him, "Behold thy mother," it was as though He had said, Let her be to thee as thine own mother; Let thy love for Me be now manifested in thy tender regard for her. Yet there was far more behind this act of Christ than that.

Of old it had been predicted that the Lord Jesus should act wisely and discreetly. Through Isaiah, God had said, "Behold, my servant shall deal prudently" (52:13). In commending His mother to the care of His loved apostle, the Saviour displayed wise discrimination in His choice of the one who was henceforth to be her guardian. Perhaps there was none who understood the Lord Jesus so well as His mother, and it is almost certain that none had apprehended His love so deeply as had John. We see therefore how they would be *fit* companions for each other, inasmuch as there was an intimate bond of common sympathy uniting them together and uniting them to Christ! Thus there was none other so well suited to take care of Mary, none whose company she would find so congenial, and on the other hand, there was none whose fellowship John would more enjoy.

Furthermore, it needs to be borne in mind that a wondrous and honorous work was waiting for John. Years later, the Lord Jesus was to reveal Himself to this apostle in glorious apocalypse. How better, then, could he equip himself for this than by being constantly with her who had lived in closest intimacy and intercourse with the Saviour during the thirty years *He had*

65

waited for the time to come when His work should begin! We can therefore see that there was a significant appropriateness in bringing these two—Mary and John—together. Admire, then, the prudence of Christ's election of a home for Mary, and at the same time providing a companion for the disciple whom He loved with whom he might have blessed spiritual fellowship.

Ere passing to our next point, we may remark that this taking of Mary into his home throws light on an incident recorded in the next chapter of John's Gospel. In John 20 we learn of the visit of Peter and John to the empty sepulchre. John outran his companion and arrived first at the tomb but went not in. Peter, characteristically, goes into the sepulchre and notes the orderly arrangement of the clothes. Then enters John and he sees and "believed," for up to this time their faith had not grasped the promises of Christ's resurrection. Consequent on John's believing, we read, "Then the disciples went away again *unto their own home*" (John 20:10). We are not told *why* they did this, but in view of John 19:27 the explanation is obvious. There we are told that "from that hour that disciple took her *unto his own home*," and now that he has learned the Saviour is risen from the dead, he hastens back "home" to tell *her* the good news! Who more than she would rejoice at the glad tidings! This is another example of the silent and hidden harmonies of Scripture.

5. Here we see that spiritual relationships must not ignore the responsibilities of nature.

The Lord Jesus was dying as the Saviour for sinners. He was engaged in the most momentous and the most stupendous undertaking that this earth ever has or ever will witness. He was on the point of offering satisfaction to the outraged justice of God. He was just about to do that work for which the world had been made, for which the human race had been created, for which all the ages had waited, and for which He, the eternal Word, had become incarnate. Nevertheless, He doesn't overlook the responsibilities of natural ties; He fails not to make provision for her who, according to the flesh, was His mother.

There is a lesson here that many need to take to heart in these days. No duty, no work, however important it may be, can *excuse* us from discharging the obligations of nature, from caring for those who have fleshly claims upon us. They who go forth as missionaries to labor in heathen lands, and who leave their children behind, or who send them back to the homeland, to be cared for by *strangers*, are not following the steps of the Saviour. Those women who spend most of their time at public meetings, even though they be religious meetings, or who go down into the slums to minister to the poor and needy, to the *neglect* of their own family at home, do but bring reproach upon the name and cause of Christ. Those men, even though they stand at the forefront of Christian work, who are so busy preaching and teaching that they have *no time* to discharge the obligations that they owe to *their own* wives and children, need to study and practice the principle exemplified here by Christ on the Cross.

6. Here we see a universal need exemplified.

How different is the Mary of Scripture from the Mary of superstition! She was no proud Madonna but, like each of us, a member of a fallen race, a sinner both by nature and practice. Before the birth of Christ, she declared, "My soul doth magnify the Lord, and my spirit hath rejoiced in God *my Saviour*" (Luke 1:46–47, emphasis added). And now at the death of the Lord Jesus, she is found before the Cross. The Word of God presents not the mother of Jesus as the queen of angels decked with diadem but as one who herself rejoiced in a Saviour. It is true she is "blessed among [not above] women," and that by virtue of the high honor of being the mother of the Redeemer; yet was she human, a real member of our fallen race, a sinner needing a Saviour.

She stood by the Cross. And as she stood there, the Saviour exclaimed, "Woman, *behold* thy son!" (John 19:26, emphasis added). There, summed up in a single word, is expressed the *need* of every descendent of Adam—to turn the eye away from the world, off from self, and to look by faith to the Saviour who died for sinners. There is the divine epitome of the way of salvation. Deliverance from the wrath to come, forgiveness of sins, acceptance with God, is obtained not by deed of merit, not by good works, not by religious ordinances. No, salvation comes by beholding—"Behold *the Lamb of God* which taketh away the sin of the world." Just as the serpent-bitten Israelites in the wilderness were healed by a look, by a look at that which Jehovah had appointed to be the object of their faith, so today, redemption from the guilt and power of sin, emancipation from the curse of the broken law and from the captivity of Satan, is to be found alone by faith in Christ, "As Moses lifted up the serpent in the wilderness, even so must the Son of man be lifted up: that *whosoever believeth in him* should not perish, but have eternal life" (John 3:14–15, emphasis added). There is life in a look. Reader, have you thus *beheld* that divine sufferer? Have you seen Him dying on the Cross, the just for the unjust, that He might bring us to God? Mary, the mother of Christ, needed to "behold" Him, and so do *you*. Then look, look unto Christ and be ye saved.

7. Here we see the marvelous blending of Christ's perfections.

This is one of the greatest wonders of His person—the blending of the most perfect human affection with His divine glory. The very Gospel that most of all shows Him to be God is here careful to prove He was man—the Word made flesh. Engaged as He was in a divine transaction, making atonement for all the sins of all His people, grappling with the powers of darkness, yet amid it all, He has still the same human tenderness, which shows the perfection of the man Jesus Christ.

This care for His mother in His dying hour was characteristic of all His conduct. Everything was natural and perfect. The unstudied simplicity about Him is most marked. There was nothing pompous or ostentatious. Many of His mightiest works were done on the highway, in the cottage, or among a little group of sufferers. Many of His words, which today are still unfathomable and exhaustless in their wealth of meaning, were uttered almost casually as He walked with a few friends. So it was at the Cross. He was performing the mightiest work of all history; He was engaged in doing that which in comparison makes the creating of a world fade into utter insignificance, yet He forgets not to make provision for His mother—much as He might have done had they been together in the home at Nazareth. Rightly was it said of old, "His name shall be called *Wonderful*" (Isa. 9:6, emphasis added). Wonderful He was in all that He did. Wonderful He was in every relationship that He sustained. Wonderful He was in His person, and wonderful He was in His work. Wonderful was He in life, and wonderful was He in death. Let *us* wonder and adore.

4

The Word of Anguish

And about the ninth hour Jesus cried with a loud voice, saying, Eli, Eli, lama sabachthani? that is to say, My God, my God, why hast thou forsaken me?

Matthew 27:46

"My God, my God, why hast thou forsaken me?"

These are words of startling import. The crucifixion of the Lord of Glory was the most extraordinary event that has ever happened on earth, and this cry of the suffering One was the most startling utterance of that appalling scene. That innocence should be condemned, that the guiltless should be persecuted, that a benefactor should be cruelly put to death, was no new event in history. From the murder of righteous Abel to that of Zecharias, there was a long list of such martyrdoms. But He who hung on this central cross was no ordinary man, He was the Son of Man, the One in whom all excellencies met—the Perfect One. Like His robe, His character was "without seam, *woven from the top throughout*."

71

In the case of all other persecuted ones, there were demerits and blemishes that might afford their murderers something to blame. But the judge of this one said, "I find *no fault* in Him." And more. This sufferer was not only perfect man, but He was the Son of God. Yet it is not strange that man should wish to destroy God. "The fool hath said in his heart, There is no God" (Ps. 14:1); such is his wish. But *it is strange* that He who was God manifest in the flesh should allow Himself to be so treated by His enemies. It is *exceeding strange* that the Father who delighted in Him, whose own voice had declared from the opened heavens, "This is my beloved Son, in whom I am well pleased" (Matt. 3:17), should deliver Him up to such a shameful death.

"My God, my God, why hast thou forsaken me?"

These are words of appalling woe. The very word "forsaken" is one of the most tragic in all human speech. The writer will not readily forget his sensation as he once passed through a town deserted of all its inhabitants—a forsaken city. What calamities are conjured up by this word—a man forsaken of his friends, a wife forsaken by her husband, a child forsaken by its parents! But a creature forsaken by its Creator, a man forsaken of God—O this is the most frightful of all. This is the evil of all evils. This is the climacteric calamity. True, fallen man, in his unrenewed condition, does not so deem it. But he, who in some measure at least, has learned that God is the sum of all perfection, the fount and goal of all excellency, he whose cry is "As the heart panteth after the water brooks, so panteth my soul after thee, O God" (Ps. 42:1), is ready to endorse what has just been said. The cry of saints in all ages has been, "Forsake us not, O God." For the Lord to hide *His* face from us but for a moment is unbearable. If this is true of renewed sinners, how infinitely more so of the beloved Son of the Father!

He who hung there on the accursed Tree had been from all eternity the object of the Father's love. To employ the language of Proverbs 8:30, the suffering Saviour was the One who "was by him, as one brought up with him," He was "daily his delight." His own joy had been to behold the Father's countenance. The Father's presence had been His home, the Father's bosom His dwelling place, the Father's glory He had shared before ever the world was. During the thirty and three years the Son had been on earth, He enjoyed unbroken communion with the Father. Never a thought that was out of harmony with the Father's mind, never a violition but what originated in the Father's will, never a moment spent out of His conscious presence. What, then, must it have meant to be *"forsaken"* now by God! Ah, the hiding of *God's face* from Him was the most bitter ingredient of that cup that the Father had given the Redeemer to drink.

"My God, my God, why hast thou forsaken me?"

These are words of unequaled pathos. They mark the climax of His sufferings. The soldiers had cruelly mocked Him: they had arrayed Him with the crown of thorns; they had scourged and buffeted Him; they even went so far as to spit upon Him and pluck off His hair. They despoiled Him of His garments and put Him to an open shame. Yet He suffered it all in silence. They pierced His hands and His feet, yet did He endure the Cross, despising the shame. The vulgar crowd taunted Him, and the thieves who were crucified with Him flung the same taunts into His face; yet He opened not His mouth. In response to all that He suffered at the hands of men, not a cry escaped His lips. But now, as the concentrated wrath of heaven descends upon Him, He cries, "My God, my God, why hast thou forsaken me?" Surely this is a cry that ought to melt the hardest heart!

"My God, my God, why hast thou forsaken me?"

These are words of deepest mystery. Of old the Lord Jehovah forsook not His people. Again and again He was their refuge in trouble. When the Israelites were in cruel bondage, they cried unto God, and He heard them. When they stood helpless before the Red Sea, He came to their aid and delivered them from their enemies. When the three Hebrews were cast into the fiery furnace, the Lord was with them. But here, at the Cross, there ascends a more plaintive and agonizing cry than ever went up from the land of Egypt, yet was there no response! Here was a situation far more alarming than the Red Sea crisis: enemies more relentless beset this One, yet was there no deliverance! Here was a fire that burned infinitely fiercer than Nebuchadnezzar's furnace, but there was no one by His side to comfort! He is abandoned by God!

Yes, this cry of the suffering Saviour is deeply mysterious. At first He had cried, "Father, forgive them, for they know not what they do," and this we can understand, for it well accords with His compassionate heart. Again had He opened His mouth, to say to the repentant thief, "Verily I say unto thee, today shalt thou be with me in paradise," and this too we can well understand, for it was in full keeping with His grace toward sinners. Once more His lips moved—to His mother, "Woman, behold thy son"; to the beloved John, "Behold thy mother"—and this also we can appreciate. But the next time He opens His mouth, a cry is made that startles and staggers us. Of old David said, "I have never seen the righteous forsaken," but here we behold the Righteous One forsaken.

"My God, my God, why hast thou forsaken me?"

These are words of profoundest solemnity. This was a cry that made the very earth tremble and that reverberated throughout the entire universe. Ah, what mind is sufficient for contemplating this wonder of wonders! What mind is capable of analyzing the meaning of this amazing cry that rent the awful darkness! "Why hast thou forsaken me?" are words that conduct us into

74

the Holy of Holies. Here, if anywhere, it is supremely fitting that we remove the shoes of carnal inquisitiveness. Speculation is profane: we can but wonder and worship.

But though these words are of startling import, appalling woe, deepest mystery, unique pathos, and profound solemnity, yet are we not left in ignorance as to their meaning. True, this cry was deeply mysterious, yet is it capable of most blessed solution. The Holy Scriptures leave it impossible to doubt that these words of unequaled grief were both the fullest manifestation of divine love and the most awe-inspiring display of God's inflexible justice. May every thought be now brought into captivity to Christ and may our hearts be duly solemnized as we take a closer view of this fourth utterance of the dying Saviour.

"My God, my God, why hast thou forsaken me?"

1. Here we see the awfulness of sin and the character of its wages.

The Lord Jesus was crucified at midday, and in the light of Calvary everything was revealed in its true character. There the very nature of things was fully and finally exhibited. The depravity of the human heart—its hatred of God, its base ingratitude, its loving of darkness rather than light, its preference of a murderer for the Prince of Life—was fearfully displayed. The awful character of the devil—his hostility against God, his insatiable enmity against Christ, his power to put it into the heart of man to betray the Saviour—was completely exposed. So too the perfections of the divine nature—God's ineffable holiness, His inflexible justice, His terrible wrath, His matchless grace—were fully made known. And there it was also that sin—its baseness, its turpitude, its lawlessness—was plainly exhibited. Here we are shown the fearful lengths to which sin will go. In its first manifestation it took the form of suicide, for Adam destroyed his own spiritual life; next we see it in the form of fratricide—Cain slaying his own brother; but at the Cross the climax is reached in deicide—man crucifying the Son of God.

But not only do we see the heinousness of sin at the Cross, but there we also discover the character of its awful wages. "The wages of sin is death" (Rom. 6:23). Death is the entail of sin. "By one man sin entered into the world, and death by sin; and so death passed upon all men, for that all have sinned" (Rom. 5:12). Had there been no sin, there would have been no death. But what is "death"? Is it that dreadful silence that reigns supreme after the last breath is drawn and the body lies motionless? Is it that ghastly pallor that comes over the face as the blood ceases to circulate and the eyes remain expressionless? Yes, it is that, but much more. Something far more pathetic and tragic than physical dissolution is contained in the term. The wages of sin is *spiritual* death. Sin separates from God, who is the fount of all life. This was shown forth in Eden. Previous to the fall, Adam enjoyed blessed fellowship with his Maker, but in the early eve of that day that marked the entrance of sin into our world, as the Lord God entered the garden and His voice was heard by our first parents, the guilty pair *hid* themselves among the trees of the garden. No longer might they enjoy communion with Him who is always light; instead, they are *alienated* from Him. So too was it with Cain: when interrogated by the Lord he said, "*From thy face* shall I be hid" (Gen. 4:14, emphasis added). Sin excludes from God's presence. That was the great lesson taught Israel. Jehovah's throne was in their midst, yet was it not accessible. He abode between the cherubim in the Holy of Holies and into it none might come, saving the high priest, and he but one day in the year bearing blood with him. The veil that hung both in the tabernacle and in the temple, barring access to the throne of God, witnessed to the solemn fact that sin *separates* from Him.

The wages of sin is death, not only physical but spiritual death; not merely natural but, essentially, *penal death*. What is physical death? It is the separation of soul and spirit from the body. So penal death is the separation of the soul and spirit from God. The Word of Truth speaks of her that lives in pleasure as being "*dead* while she liveth" (1 Tim. 5:6, emphasis added). Note too how that wonderful parable of the prodigal son illustrates the force of the term "death." After the return of the prodigal, the father said, "This my son was *dead*, and is alive again; he was lost, and is found" (Luke 15:24, emphasis added). While he was in the "far country" he had not ceased to exist; no, he was dead not physically but spiritually—he was alienated and separated from his father!

Now on the Cross the Lord Jesus was receiving the wages that were due His people. He had no sin of His own, for He was the Holy One of God. But He was bearing *our* sins in His own body on the Tree (1 Pet. 2:24). He had taken our place and was suffering, the just for the unjust. He was bearing the chastisement of our peace; and the wages of our sins, the suffering and chastisement that were due us, was "death." Not merely physical but penal; and as we have said, this meant separation from God, and hence it was that the Saviour cried, "My God, my God, why hast thou forsaken me?"

So too will it be with the finally impenitent. The awful doom awaiting the lost is thus set forth—"Who shall be punished with everlasting destruction *from the presence of the Lord*, and from the glory of his power" (2 Thess. 1:9, emphasis added). Eternal separation from Him who is the fount of all goodness and the source of all blessing. Unto the wicked Christ shall say, "*Depart from me*, ye cursed"—banishment from His presence, an eternal exile from God, is what awaits the damned. This is the reason the Lake of Fire—the eternal abode of those whose names are not written in the Book of Life—is designated "*the second death*" (Rev. 20:14, emphasis added). Not that there will be extinction of being but everlasting separation from the Lord of life, a separation that Christ suffered for three hours as He hung in the sinner's place. At the Cross, then, Christ received the wages of sin.

"My God, my God, why hast thou forsaken me?"

77

2. Here we see the absolute holiness and inflexible justice of God.

The tragedy of Calvary must be viewed from at least four different viewpoints. At the Cross *man* did a work: he displayed his depravity by taking the Perfect One and with "wicked hands" nailing Him to the Tree. At the Cross *Satan* did a work: he manifested his insatiable enmity against the woman's seed by bruising His heel. At the Cross *the Lord Jesus* did a work: He died, the just for the unjust, that He might bring us to God. At the Cross God did a work: He exhibited His holiness and satisfied His justice by pouring out His wrath on the One who was made sin for us.

What human pen is able or fit to write about the unsullied *holiness* of God! So holy is God that mortal man cannot look upon Him in His essential being and live. So holy is God that the very heavens are not clean in His sight. So holy is God that even the seraphim veil their faces before Him. So holy is God that when Abraham stood before Him, he cried, "[I] am but dust and ashes" (Gen. 18:27). So holy is God that when Job came into His presence, he said, "Wherefore I abhor myself" (Job 42:6). So holy is God that when Isaiah had a vision of His glory, he exclaimed, "Woe is me! for I am undone . . . for mine eyes have seen the King, the LORD of hosts" (Isa. 6:5). So holy is God that when Daniel beheld Him in theophanic manifestation, he declared, "there remained no strength in me; for my comeliness was turned in me into corruption" (Dan. 10:8). So holy is God that we are told, "[He is] of purer eyes than to behold evil, and canst not look on iniquity" (Hab. 1:13). And it was because the Saviour was bearing our sins that the thrice holy God would not look on Him, turned His face from Him, forsook Him. The Lord made to meet on Christ the iniquities of us all: and our sins being on Him as our substitute, the divine wrath against our offenses must be spent upon our sin offering.

"My God, my God, why hast thou forsaken me?" That

was a question that none of those around the Cross could have answered; it was a question that, at that time, none of the apostles could have answered; yea, it was a question that had puzzled the angels in heaven to make reply to. But the Lord Jesus had answered His own question, and His answer is found in Psalm 22. This psalm furnished a most wonderful prophetic foreview of His sufferings. The psalm opens with the very words of our Saviour's fourth cross utterance, and it is followed by further agonizing sobs in the same strain till, at verse 3 we find Him saying—"But thou art holy." He complains not of injustice; instead, He acknowledges God's righteousness—Thou art holy and just in exacting all the debt at My hand that I am surety for; I have all the sins of all My people to answer for, and therefore I justify Thee, O God, in giving Me this stroke from Thine awakened sword. Thou art Holy: Thou art clear when Thou judgest.

At the Cross, then, as nowhere else, we see the infinite malignity of sin and the justice of God in the punishment thereof. Was the old world overflown with water? Were Sodom and Gomorrah destroyed by a storm of fire and brimstone? Were the plagues sent upon Egypt and was Pharaoh and his hosts drowned in the Red Sea? In these may the demerit of sin and God's hatred thereof be seen, but much more so here is Christ forsaken of God. Go to Golgotha and see the man that is Jehovah's fellow drinking up the cup of His Father's indignation, smitten by the sword of divine justice, brushed by the Lord Himself, suffering unto death, for God "spared not his own Son" when He hung in the sinner's place.

Behold how nature herself had anticipated the dreadful tragedy—the very contour of the ground is like unto a *skull*. Behold the earth trembling beneath the mighty load of outpoured wrath. Behold the heavens as the sun turns away from such a scene and the land is covered with darkness. Here may we see the dreadful anger of a sin-avenging God. Not all the thunderbolts of divine judgment that were let loose in Old Testament times, not all the vials of wrath that shall yet be poured forth on an apostate Christendom during the unparalleled horrors of the Great Tribulation, not all the weeping and wailing and gnashing of teeth of the damned in the Lake of Fire ever gave, or ever will give, such a demonstration of God's inflexible justice and ineffable holiness, of His infinite hatred of sin, as did the wrath of God that flamed against His own Son on the Cross. Because He was enduring sin's terrific judgment, He was forsaken of God. He who was the Holy One, whose *own* abhorrence of sin was infinite, who was purity incarnate (1 John 3:3) was made sin for us (2 Cor. 5:21); therefore did He bow before the storm of wrath, in which was displayed the divine displeasure against the countless sins of a great multitude whom no man can number. This, then, is the true explanation of Calvary. God's holy character could not do less than *judge* sin even though it be found on Christ Himself. At the Cross, then, God's justice was satisfied and His holiness vindicated.

"My God, my God, why hast thou forsaken me?"

3. Here we see the explanation of Gethsemane.

As our blessed Lord approached the Cross, the horizon darkened for Him more and more. From earliest infancy He had suffered from *man*; from the beginning of His public ministry, He had suffered from *Satan*; but at the Cross He was to suffer at the hand of *God*. Jehovah Himself was to bruise the Saviour, and it was *this* that overshadowed everything else. In Gethsemane He entered the gloom of the three hours of darkness on the Cross. That is why He left the three disciples on the outskirts of the garden, for He must tread the winepress alone. "My soul is exceeding sorrowful," He cried. This was no shrinking horror in anticipation of a cruel death. It was not the thought of betrayal by His own familiar friend, nor of desertion by His cherished disciples in the hour of crisis, nor was it the expectation of the mockings and revilings, the stripes and the nails, that overwhelmed His soul. No, all of this keenest anguish, as it must have been to His sensitive spirit, was as nothing compared with what He had to endure as the Sin Bearer.

"Then cometh Jesus with them unto a place called Gethsemane, and saith unto the disciples, Sit ye here, while I go and pray yonder. And he took with him Peter and the two sons of Zebedee, and began to be sorrowful and very heavy. Then saith he unto them, My soul is exceeding sorrowful, even unto death: tarry ye here, and watch with me. And he went a little farther, and fell on his face, and prayed, saying, O my Father, if it be possible, let this cup pass from me: nevertheless not as I will, but as thou wilt" (Matt. 26:36–39). Here He views the black clouds arising. He sees the dreadful storm coming; He premeditated the inexpressible horror of that three hours of darkness and all they held. "My soul is exceeding sorrowful," He cries. The Greek is most emphatic. He was begirt with sorrow. He was plunged over head and ears in the anticipated wrath of God. All the faculties and powers of His soul were wrung with anguish. St. Mark employs another form of expression—He "began to be sore amazed" (14:33). The original signifies the greatest extremity of amazement, such as makes one's hair stand on end and his flesh to creep. Mark adds, "and to be very heavy," which denotes there was an utter sinking of spirit; His heart was melted like wax at the sight of the terrible cup. But the evangelist Luke uses the strongest terms of all: "And being in an agony he prayed more earnestly: and his sweat was as it were great drops of blood falling down to the ground" (Luke 22:44). The Greek word for "agony" here means to be engaged in a combat. Before, He had combated the oppositions of men and the oppositions of the Devil, but now He faces the cup that God gives Him to drink. It was the cup that contained the undiluted wrath of a sin-hating God. This explains why He said, "If it be possible, let *this* cup pass from me." The "cup" is the symbol of communion, and there could be no communion in His wrath but only in His love. Notwithstanding, though it means being cut off from communion. He adds, "Nevertheless not as I will, but as thou wilt." Yet so great was His agony that "his sweat was as it were great drops of blood falling down to the ground." We think that there can be little doubt that the Saviour shed actual drops of blood. There would be little meaning in saying that His sweat *resembled* blood but *was not* really that. It seems to us the emphasis is on the word "blood." He shed *blood*—just like great beads of water in *ordinary* cases. And here we see the fitness of the place chosen to be the scene of this terrible but preliminary suffering. "Gethsemane"—ah, thy name betrayeth thee! It means the olive press. It was the place where the lifeblood of the olives was pressed out drop by drop! The chosen place was well named, then. It was indeed a fit footstool to the Cross, a footstool of agony unutterable and unparalleled. On the Cross, then, Christ drained the cup that was presented to Him in Gethsemane.

"My God, my God, why hast thou forsaken me?"

4. Here we see the Saviour's unswerving fidelity to God.

The forsaking of the Redeemer by God was a solemn fact, and an experience that left Him nothing but the supports of His *faith*. Our Saviour's position on the Cross was absolutely unique. This may readily be seen by contrasting His own words spoken during His public ministry with those uttered on the Cross itself. Formerly He said, "And I knew that *thou hearest me always*" (John 11:42, emphasis added); now He cries, "O my God, I cry in the daytime, *but thou hearest not*" (Ps. 22:2, emphasis added)! Formerly He said, "And he that sent me is with me: *the Father hath not left me alone*" (John 8:29, emphasis added); now He cries, "My God, my God, *why hast thou forsaken me?*" He had absolutely nothing now to rest upon save His Father's covenant and promise; and in His cry of anguish His father is made manifest. It was a cry of distress but not of distrust. God had withdrawn from Him, but mark how His soul still cleaves to God. His faith triumphed by laying hold of God even amid the darkness. "*My God,*" He says, "My God," Thou with whom is infinite and everlasting strength; Thou who hast hitherto supported my manhood, and according to Thy promise upheld Thy servant—O be not far from Me now. My God, I lean on Thee. When all visible and sensible comforts had disappeared, to the invisible support and refuge of His faith did the Saviour betake Himself.

In the twenty-second Psalm, the Saviour's unswerving fidelity to God is most apparent. In this precious psalm the depths of His heart are told out. Hear Him: "Our fathers trusted in thee: they trusted, and thou didst deliver them. They cried unto thee, and were delivered: they trusted in thee, and were not confounded. But I am a worm, and no man; a reproach of men, and despised of the people. All they that see me laugh me to scorn: they shoot out the lip, they shake the head, saying, He trusted on the LORD that he would deliver him: let him deliver him, seeing he delighted in him. But thou art he that took me out of the womb: thou didst make me hope when I was upon my mother's breasts. I was cast upon thee from the womb: thou art my God from my mother's belly" (Ps. 22:4–10). The very point His enemies sought to make against Him was His faith in God. They taunted Him with His "trust" in Jehovah—if He *really* trusted in the Lord, the Lord would deliver Him. But the Saviour *continued trusting* though there was *no* deliverance, trusted though "forsaken" for a season! He had been cast upon God from the womb, and He is still found cast upon God in the hour of His death. He continues, "Be not far from me; for trouble is near; for there is none to help. Many bulls have compassed me: strong bulls of Bashan have beset me round. They gaped upon me with their mouths, as a ravening and a roaring lion. I am poured out like water, and all my bones are out of joint: my heart is like wax; it is melted in the midst of my bowels. My strength is dried up like a potsherd; and my tongue cleaveth to my jaws; and thou hast brought me into the dust of death. For dogs have compassed me: the assembly of the wicked have inclosed me: they pierced my hands and my feet. I may tell all my bones: they look and stare upon me.

They part my garments among them, and cast lots upon my vesture. But be not thou far from me, O LORD; O my strength, haste thee to help me. Deliver my soul from the sword; my darling from the power of the dog" (Ps. 22:11–20). Job had said of God, "Though he slay me, yet will I trust in him" (Job 13:15). And though the wrath of God against sin rested upon Christ, still He trusted. Yea, His faith did more than trust; it triumphed—"Save me from the lion's mouth: for thou hast heard me from the horns of the unicorns" (Ps. 22:21).

O what an example has the Saviour left His people! It is comparatively easy to trust God while the sun is shining; the test comes when all is dark. But a faith that does not rest on God in adversity as well as in prosperity is not the faith of God's elect: We must have faith to live by—true faith—if we would have faith to die by. The Saviour had been cast upon God from His mother's womb, had been cast upon God moment by moment all through those thirty-three years; what wonder, then, that the hour of death finds Him still cast upon God. Fellow Christian, all may be dark with thee; you may no longer behold the light of God's countenance. Providence seems to frown upon you; notwithstanding, say still Eli, Eli, My God, My God.

"My God, my God, why hast thou forsaken me?"

5. Here we may see the basis of our salvation.

God is holy, and therefore He will not look upon sin. God is just, and therefore He judges sin wherever it is found. But God is Love as well: God delighteth in mercy, and therefore infinite wisdom devised a way whereby justice might be satisfied and mercy left free to flow out to guilty sinners. This way was the way of substitution, the just suffering for the unjust. The Son of God Himself was the One selected to be the substitute, for none other would suffice. Through Nahum, the question had been asked, "*Who can stand* before his indignation? and *who* can abide in the fierceness of his anger?" (1:6, emphasis added).

This question received its answer in the adorable person of our Lord and Saviour Jesus Christ. He alone could "stand." One only could bear the curse and yet rise a victor above it. One only could endure all the avenging wrath and yet magnify the law and make it honorable. One only could suffer His heel to be bruised by Satan and yet in that bruising destroy him that had the power of death. God laid hold upon One that was *mighty* (Ps. 89:19), One who was no less than the fellow of Jehovah, the radiance of His glory, the exact impress of His person. Thus we see that boundless love, inflexible justice, and omnipotent power all combined to make possible the salvation of those who believe.

At the Cross all our iniquities were laid upon Christ and therefore did divine judgment fall upon Him. There was no way of transferring sin without also transferring its penalty. Both sin and its punishment were transferred to the Lord Jesus. On the Cross Christ was making propitiation, and propitiation is solely *Godward*. It was a question of meeting the claims of God's holiness; it was a matter of satisfying the demands of His justice. Not only was Christ's blood shed for *us*, but it was also shed for *God*: He "hath given himself for us an offering and a sacrifice *to God* for a sweetsmelling savour" (Eph. 5:2, emphasis added). Thus it was foreshadowed on the memorable night of the Passover in Egypt: the lamb's blood must be where God's eye could see it—"When I see the blood, I will pass over you!"

The death of Christ on the Cross was a death of curse: "Christ hath redeemed us from the curse of the law, being made a curse for us: for it is written, Cursed is every one that hangeth on a tree" (Gal. 3:13). The "curse" is alienation from God. This is apparent from the words that Christ will yet speak to those who shall stand on His left hand in the day of His power—"Depart from me, ye cursed" He will say (Matt. 25:41). The curse is *exile* from the presence and glory of God. This explains the meaning of a number of Old Testament types. The bullock that was slain on the annual Day of Atonement, after its blood had been sprinkled upon and before the mercy seat, was removed to a place *without (outside) the camp* (Lev. 16:27) and there its entire carcass was burned. It was in the center of the camp that God had His dwelling place, and exclusion from the camp was banishment from the presence of God. Thus it was too with the leper. "All the days wherein the plague shall be in him he shall be defiled; he is unclean: he shall dwell alone; *without the camp shall his habitation be*" (Lev. 13:46, emphasis added)—this because the leper was the embodied type of the sinner. Here also is the antitype of the "brazen serpent." Why did God instruct Moses to set a "serpent" on a pole and bid the bitten Israelites look upon it? Imagine a *serpent* as a type of Christ, the Holy One of God! Yes, but it represented Him as "made a *curse* for us," for the serpent was the reminder of the curse. On the Cross, then, Christ was fulfilling these Old Testament foreshadowings. He was "outside the camp" (compare Heb. 13:12)—separated from the presence of God. He was as the "leper"—made sin for us. He was as the "brazen serpent"—made a curse for us. Hence too the deep meaning of the crown of thorns—the symbol of the curse! Lifted up, His brow encircled with thorns, to show He was bearing the curse for us.

Here too is the significance of the three hours darkness that lay over the land as a pall of death. It was supernatural darkness. It was not night, for the sun was at its zenith. As Mr. Spurgeon well said, "It was midnight at midday." It was no eclipse. Competent astronomers tell us that at the time of the crucifixion the moon was at her farthest from the sun. But this cry of Christ's gives the meaning of the darkness, as the darkness gives us the meaning of that bitter cry. One thing alone can explain this darkness, as one thing alone can interpret this cry—that Christ had taken the place of guilty and lost ones, that He was in the place of sin bearing, that He was enduring the judgment due His people, that He who knew no sin was "made sin" for us. That cry was uttered that we might be allowed to know of what passed there. It was the *manifestation* of atonement, so to speak, for three (three hours) is ever the number of manifestation. God is Light and the "darkness" is the natural sign of His turning away. The Redeemer was left *alone* with the sinner's sin: that was the explanation of the three hours darkness. Just as there will rest upon the damned a twofold misery in the lake of fire, namely, the pain of sense and the pain of loss; so upon Christ answerably, He suffered the outpoured wrath of God and also the withdrawal of His presence and fellowship.

For the believer the Cross is interpreted in Galatians 2:20—"I am crucified with Christ." He was my substitute; God reckoned me one with the Saviour. His death was mine. He was wounded for *my* transgressions and bruised for *my* iniquities. Sin was not pushed away but put away. As another has said, "Because God judged sin *on* the Son, He now accepts the believing sinner *in* the Son." Our life is hid with Christ in God (Col. 3:3). I am shut up in Christ because Christ was shut out from God.

> He suffered in our stead, He saved His people thus;
> The Curse that fell upon His head was due by right to us.
> The storm that bowed His blessed head is hushed for ever
> now
> And rest Divine is mine instead, while glory crowns His
> brow.

Here, then, is the basis of our salvation. Our sins have been borne. God's claims against us have been fully met. Christ was forsaken of God for a season that we might enjoy His presence forever. "My God, my God, why hast thou forsaken me?" Let every believing soul make answer: He entered the awful darkness that I might walk in the light; He drank the cup of woe that I might drink the cup of joy; He was forsaken that I might be forgiven!

"My God, my God, why hast thou forsaken me?"

6. Here we see the supreme evidence of Christ's love for us.

"Greater love hath no man than this, that a man lay down his life for his friends" (John 15:13). But the greatness of *Christ's* love can be estimated only when we are able to measure what was involved in the "laying down" of *His* love. As we have seen, it meant much more than physical death, even though that be of unspeakable shame and indescribable suffering. It meant that He take our place and be "made sin" for us, and what *this* involved can only be judged in the light of His *person*. Picture a perfectly honorable and virtuous woman compelled to endure for a season association with the vilest and impurest. Imagine her shut up in a den of iniquity, surrounded by the coarsest of all men and women, and with no way of escape. Can you estimate her abhorrence of the foul-mouthed oaths, the drunken revelry, and obscene surroundings? Can you form an opinion of what a pure woman would suffer in her soul amid such impurity? But the illustration falls far short, for there is no woman absolutely pure—honorable, virtuous, morally pure. Yes, but pure in the sense of being sinless, spiritually pure. No. But Christ *was* pure, absolutely pure. He was the Holy One. He had an infinite abhorrence of sin. He loathed it. His holy soul shrank from it. But on the Cross our iniquities were all laid upon Him, and sin—that vile thing—enrapt itself around Him like a horrible serpent's coils. And yet He willingly suffered for us! Why? Because He *loved* us: "Having loved his own which were in the world, he loved them unto the end" (John 13:1).

But more: the greatness of Christ's love for us can be estimated only when we are able to measure the wrath of God that was poured upon Him. This it was from which His soul shrank. What *this* meant to Him, what it cost Him, may be learned in part by a perusal of the Psalms in which we are permitted to hear some of His pathetic soliloguisings and petitions to God. Speaking anticipatively, the Lord Jesus Himself by the Spirit cried through David, "Save me, O God; for the waters are come in unto my soul. I sink in deep mire, where there is no standing: I am come into deep waters, where the floods overflow me. I am weary of my crying: my throat is dried: mine eyes fail while I wait for my God . . . Deliver me out of the mire, and let me not sink: let me be delivered from them that hate me, and out of the deep waters. Let not the waterflood overflow me, neither let the deep swallow me up, and let not the pit shut her mouth upon me . . . hide not thy face from thy servant; for I am in trouble: hear me speedily. Draw nigh unto my soul, and redeem it: deliver me because of mine enemies. Thou hast known my reproach, and my shame, and my dishonour: mine adversaries are all before thee. Reproach hath broken my heart; and I am full of heaviness: and I looked for some to take pity, but there was none; and for comforters, but I found none" (Ps. 69:1–3, 14–15, 17–20). And again, "Deep calleth unto deep at the noise of thy waterspouts: all thy waves and thy billows are gone over me" (Ps. 42:7). God's abhorrence of sin swept forth and broke like a descending deluge upon the Sin Bearer. Looking forward to the awful anguish of the Cross, He cried through Jeremiah, "Is it nothing to you, all ye that pass by? behold, and see if there be any sorrow like unto my sorrow, which is done unto me, wherewith *the* LORD hath afflicted me in the day of *his fierce anger*" (Lam. 1:12, emphasis added). These are a few of the intimations we have by which we can judge of the unspeakable horror with which the Holy One contemplated those three hours on the Cross, hours into which was condensed the equivalent of an eternal hell. The Beloved of the Father must have the light of God's countenance hidden from Him; He must be left alone in the outer darkness.

Here was love matchless and unmeasured. "If it be possible, let this cup pass from me," He cried. But it was not possible that His people should be saved unless He drained that awful cup of woe and wrath; and because there was none other who could drink it, *He* drained it. Blessed be His name! Where sin had brought men, love brought the Saviour.

"My God, my God, why hast thou forsaken me?"

7. Here we see the destruction of the "larger hope."

This cry of the Saviour's foretells the final condition of every lost soul—forsaken of God! Faithfulness compels us to warn the reader against the false teachings of the day. We are told that God loves everybody and that He is too merciful to ever carry out the threatenings of His Word. This is precisely how the old Serpent argued with Eve. God had said, "In the day that thou eatest thereof thou shalt *surely* die." The serpent said, "Ye shall *not* surely die." But whose word proved true? Not the devil's, for he is a liar from the beginning. God's threat *was* fulfilled, and our first parents died spiritually in the day that they disobeyed His command. Thus will it prove in a coming day. God *is* merciful: the fact that He has provided a Saviour, reader, proves it. The fact that He invites you to receive Christ as your Saviour evidences His mercy. The fact that He has been so long-suffering with you, has borne with your stubborn rebellion till now, has prolonged your day of grace to this moment, proves it. But there is a limit to God's mercy. The day of mercy will soon be ended. The door of hope will soon be closed fast. Death may speedily cut thee off, and after death is "the judgment." And in the day of judgment God will deal in justice and not in mercy. He will avenge the mercy you have scorned. He will execute the sentence of condemnation already passed upon you: "He that believeth not shall be damned" (Mark 16:16).

We will not repeat again what has already been said at length, sufficient now to remind the reader once more how this cry of Christ's witnesses to God's hatred of sin. Because He is holy and just, God must judge sin wherever it is found. If, then, God spared not the Lord Jesus when sin was found on Him, what possible hope is there, unsaved reader, that He will spare *thee* when thou standest before Him at the great white throne with sin upon thee? If God poured out His wrath on Christ while He hung as surety for His people, be assured that

He will most certainly pour out His wrath on *you* if you die in your sins. The word of truth is explicit—"He that believeth not the Son shall not see life; but *the wrath of God* abideth on him" (John 3:36, emphasis added). God "*spared not*" His own Son when He took the sinner's place, nor will He spare him who rejects the Saviour. Christ was separated from God for three hours, and if you finally reject Him as your Saviour, *you* will be separated from God forever—"Who shall be punished with everlasting destruction from the presence of the Lord" (2 Thess. 1:9).

"My God, my God, why hast thou forsaken me?"
Here was a Cry of Desolation—
    Reader, may you never echo it.
Here was a Cry of Separation—
    Reader, may you never experience it.
Here was a Cry of Expiration—
    Reader, may you appropriate its saving virtues.

5

The Word of Suffering

Jesus knowing that all things were now accomplished,
that the scripture might be fulfilled,
saith, I thirst.

John 19:28

"I thirst." These words were spoken by the suffering Saviour
a little before He bowed the head and gave up the spirit. They
are recorded only by the evangelist John, and as we shall see,
it is fitting they should have a place in his Gospel for they
not only evidence Christ's humanity but bring out His divine
glory too.

"I thirst." What a text for a sermon! A short one it is true,
yet how comprehensive, how expressive, and how tragic! The
Maker of heaven and earth with parched lips! The Lord of
Glory in need of a drink! The Beloved of the Father crying "I
thirst"! What a scene! What a word is this! Plainly, no unin-
spired pen drew such a picture.

Of old the Spirit of God moved David to say of the coming Messiah, "They gave me also gall for my meat; and in my

thirst they gave me vinegar to drink" (Ps. 69:21, emphasis added). How marvelously complete was the prophetic foreview! No essential item was missing from it. Every important detail of the great tragedy had been written down beforehand. The betrayal by a familiar friend (Ps. 41:9), the forsaking of the disciples through being offended at Him (Ps. 31:11), the false accusation (Ps. 35:11), the silence before His judges (Isa. 53:7), the being proven guiltless (Isa. 53:9), the numbering of Him with transgressors (Isa. 53:12), the being crucified (Ps. 22:16), the mockery of the spectators (Ps. 109:25), the taunt of nondeliverance (Ps. 22:7–8), the gambling for His garments (Ps. 22:18), the prayer for His enemies (Isa. 53:12), the being forsaken of God (Ps. 22:1), the thirsting (Ps. 69:21), the yielding of His spirit into the hands of the Father (Ps. 31:5), the bones not broken (Ps. 34:20), the burial in a rich man's tomb (Isa. 53:9)—all plainly foretold centuries before they came to pass. What a convincing evidence of the divine inspiration of the Scriptures! How firm a foundation, ye saints of the Lord, is laid for your faith in His excellent Word!

"I thirst." The fact that this is recorded as one of the seven cross utterances of our Lord intimates that it is a word of precious meaning, a word to be treasured up in our hearts, a word deserving of prolonged meditation. We have seen that each of the previous sayings of the suffering Saviour has much to teach us; surely this one can be no exception. What, then, are we to gather from it? What are the lessons that this fifth cross word teaches us? May the Spirit of Truth illumine our understanding as we endeavor to fix our attention upon it.

"I thirst."

1. Here we have an evidence of Christ's humanity.

The Lord Jesus was very God of very God, but He was also very man of very man. This is something to be believed and not for proud reasons to speculate upon. The person of our adorable Saviour is not a fit object for intellectual diagnosis;

94

rather must we bow before Him in worship. He Himself warned us, "No man knoweth the Son, but the Father" (Matt. 11:27). And again, the Spirit of God through the apostle Paul declares, "Without controversy great is the mystery of godliness: God was manifest in the flesh" (1 Tim. 3:16). While, then, there is much about the person of Christ that we cannot fathom with our own understanding, yet there is everything about Him to admire and adore: foremost are His deity and humanity, and the perfect union of these two in one person. The Lord Jesus was not a divine man, nor a humanized God; He was the God-man. Forever God, and now forever man. When the Beloved of the Father became incarnate, He did not cease to be God, nor did He lay aside any of His divine attributes, though He did strip Himself of the *glory* that He had with the Father before the world was. But in the incarnation the Word became flesh and tabernacled among men. He ceased not to be all that He was previously, but He took to Himself that which He had not before—perfect humanity.

The deity and the humanity of the Saviour were each contemplated in Messianic prediction. Prophecy represented the Coming One sometimes as divine, sometimes as human. He was the "branch of the LORD" (Isa. 4:2). He was the Wonderful Counselor, the mighty God, the Father of the ages (Hebrews), the Prince of Peace (Isa 9:6). The One who was to come forth out of Bethlehem and be ruler in Israel was One whose goings forth had been from the days of eternity (Mic. 5:2). It was none less than Jehovah Himself who was to come suddenly to the temple (Mal. 3:1). Yet, on the other hand, He was the woman's seed (Gen. 3:15); a prophet like unto Moses (Deut. 18:18); a lineal descendant of David (2 Sam. 7:12–13). He was Jehovah's "servant" (Isa. 42:1). He was "a man of sorrows" (Isa. 53:3). And it is in the New Testament we see these two different sets of prophecy harmonized.

The One born at Bethlehem was the Divine Word. The incarnation does not mean that God manifested Himself as a man. The Word became flesh; He became what He was not before, though He never ceased to be all He was previously. He who was "in the form of God, thought it not robbery to be equal with God: but made himself of no reputation, and took upon him the form of a servant, and was made in the likeness of men" (Phil. 2:6–7). The Babe of Bethlehem was Immanuel—God with us. He was more than a manifestation of God; *He was* God manifest in the flesh. He was both Son of God and Son of Man. Not two separate personalities but one Person possessing two natures—the divine and the human.

While here on earth the Lord Jesus gave full proof of His deity. He spoke with divine wisdom, He acted in divine holiness, He exhibited divine power, and He displayed divine love. He read men's minds, moved men's hearts, and compelled men's wills. When He was pleased to exert His power, all nature was subject to His bidding. A word from Him and disease fled, a storm was stilled, the Devil left Him, the dead were raised to life. So truly was He God manifest in the flesh, He could say, "He that hath seen me, hath seen the Father."

So too while He tabernacled among men, the Lord Jesus gave full proof of His humanity—sinless humanity. He entered this world as a babe and was "wrapped in swaddling clothes" (Luke 2:7). As a child, we are told, He "increased in wisdom and stature" (Luke 2:52). As a boy we find Him "asking questions" (Luke 2:46). As a man He was "wearied" in body (John 4:6). He was "an hungred" (Matt. 4:2). He "slept" (Mark 4:38). He "marveled" (Mark 6:6). He "wept" (John 11:35). He "prayed" (Mark 1:35). He "rejoiced" (Luke 10:21). He "groaned" (John 11:33). And here in our text He cried, "I thirst." That evidenced His humanity. God does not thirst. The angels do not. We shall not in glory—"They shall hunger no more, neither thirst any more" (Rev. 7:16). But we thirst now because we are human and living in a world of sorrow. And Christ thirsted because He was Man—"Wherefore in all things it behooved him to be made like unto his brethren" (Heb. 2:17).

"I thirst."

2. Here we see the intensity of Christ's sufferings.

Let us first consider this cry of the Saviour's as an expression of His bodily suffering. To realize something of what lay behind these words of His, we must recall and review what preceded them. After instituting the supper in the upper room, followed by the lengthy pascal discourse to His apostles, the Redeemer adjourned to Gethsemane, and there for an hour He passed through the most excruciating agony. His soul was exceeding sorrowful. As He contemplated the awful cup, He shed not beads of perspiration but great drops of blood. His wrestling in the garden was terminated by the appearing of the traitor accompanied by the band who had come to arrest Him. He was brought before Caiaphas, and middle of the night though it was, He was examined and condemned. The Saviour was held until early morning and, after the weary hours of waiting were over, was brought before Pilate. Following a lengthy trial, orders were given for Him to be scourged. Next He was led, perhaps right across the city, to Herod's judgment hall, and after a brief appearance before this Roman prelate, He was delivered into the hands of the brutal soldiers. Again He was mocked and scourged, and again He was led across the city, back to Pilate. Once more there was the weary delay, the formalities of a trial, if such a farce deserves the name, followed by the passing sentence of death. Then, with bleeding back, carrying His cross under the heat of the now almost midday sun, He journeyed up the rugged heights of Golgotha. Reaching the appointed place of execution, His hands and feet were nailed to the Tree. For three hours He hung there with the pitiless rays of the sun beating down on His thorn-crowned head. This was followed by the three hours of darkness, now over. That night and that day were hours into which an eternity was compressed. Yet during it all not a single word of murmuring passed His lips. There was no complaining, no begging for mercy. All His sufferings had been born in majestic silence. Like a sheep dumb before her shearers, so He opened not His mouth. But now, at the end, His whole body wracked with pain, His mouth parched, He cries, "I thirst." It was not an appeal for pity, nor a request for the alleviation of His sufferings; it gave expression to the intensity of the agonies He was undergoing.

"I thirst." This was more than ordinary thirst. There was something deeper than physical sufferings behind it. A careful comparison of our text with Matthew 27:48 shows these words "I thirst" followed immediately after the fourth of our Saviour's cross utterances—"Eli, Eli, lama sabachthani"—for while the soldier was pressing the sponge of vinegar to the sufferer's lips, some of the spectators cried out, "Let be, let us see whether Elias will come to save him" (Matt. 27:49). We all know the internal trials of the soul react upon the body, rending its nerves and affecting its strength—"A broken spirit drieth the bones" (Prov. 17:22); "When I kept silence, my bones waxed old through my roaring all the day long. For day and night thy hand was heavy upon me: my moisture is turned into the drought of summer" (Ps. 32:3–4). The body and the soul sympathize with each other. Let us remember that the Saviour had just emerged from the three hours of darkness, during which God's face had been turned away from Him as He endured the fierceness of His outpoured wrath. This cry of bodily suffering tells us, then, of the *severity* of the spiritual conflict through which He had just passed! Speaking anticipatively by the mouth of Jeremiah of this very hour, He said, "Is it nothing to you, all ye that pass by? behold, and see if there be any sorrow like unto my sorrow, which is done upon me, wherewith the LORD hath afflicted me in the day of his fierce anger. From above hath he sent fire into my bones, and it prevaileth against them: he hath spread a net for my feet, he hath turned me back: he hath made me desolate and faint" (Lam. 1:12–13). His "thirst" was *the effect* of the agony of His soul in the fierce heat of God's wrath. It told of the *drought* of the land where the living God is not. But more: it plainly expressed His yearning for communion with God again, from whom for three hours He had been separated. Was it not Christ Himself who said by the spirit of prophecy, said it now, immediately He emerged from the darkness—"As the hart panteth after the water brooks, so panteth my soul after thee, O God. *My soul thirsteth for God*, for the living God: when shall I come and appear before God?" Do not the words that follow identify the speaker and reveal the time that longing and "panting was expressed"?—"My tears have been my meat day and night, while they continually say unto me, Where is thy God?" (Ps. 42:1–3, emphasis added).

"I thirst."

3. Here we see our Lord's deep reverence for the Scriptures.

How constantly the Saviour's mind turned toward the Sacred Oracles! He lived indeed by every word that proceedeth out of the mouth of God. He was the "Blessed Man" that meditated in God's law "day and night" (Ps. 1:2). The written Word was that which formed His thoughts, filled His heart, and regulated His ways. The Scriptures are the transcript of the Father's will, and that was ever His delight. In the temptation, that which was written was His defense. In His teaching, the statutes of the Lord were His authority. In His controversies with the scribes and Pharisees, His appeal was ever to the law and the testimony. And now, in His death hour, His mind dwelt upon the Word of Truth.

In order to get the primary force of this fifth cross utterance of the Saviour, we must note its setting: "Jesus knowing that all things were now accomplished, *that the scripture might be fulfilled*, saith, I thirst" (John 19:28, emphasis added). The reference is to the sixty-ninth Psalm—another of the Messianic Psalms that describe so graphically His passion. In it the Spirit of prophecy had declared, "They gave me also gall for my meat; and in my thirst they gave me vinegar to drink" (v. 21). This remained yet unaccomplished. The predictions of the previous verses had already received fulfillment. He had sunk in the "deep mire" (v. 2); He had been hated "without a cause" (v. 4);

He had borne reproach and shame (v. 7); He had "become a stranger unto [his] brethren" (v. 8); He had become "a proverb" to His revilers, and "the song of the drunkards" (vv. 11–12); He had cried unto God in His distress (vv. 17–20)—and now there remained nothing more than offering to Him the drink of vinegar and gall, *and in order to this* He cried, "I thirst."

"*Jesus knowing that all things were now accomplished*, that the scripture might be fulfilled, saith, I thirst." How completely self-possessed the Saviour was! He had hung on that cross for six hours and had passed through unparalleled suffering, yet is His mind clear and His memory unimpaired. He had before Him, with perfect distinctness, the whole truth of God. He reviewed the entire scope of Messianic prediction. He remembers there is one prophetic Scripture unaccomplished. He overlooked nothing. What a proof is this that He was divinely superior to all circumstances!

Ere passing on, we would briefly point an application to ourselves. We have remarked how the Saviour bowed to the authority of Scripture both in life and in death—Christian reader how is it with thee? Is the Book Divine the final court of appeal with you? Do you discover in it a revelation of God's mind and will concerning *you*? Is it a lamp unto your feet? That is, are you walking in its light? Are its commands binding on you? Are you really *obeying* it? Can you say with David, "I have chosen the way of truth: thy judgments have I laid before me. I have stuck unto thy testimonies . . . I thought on my ways, and turned my feet unto thy testimonies. I made haste, and delayed not to keep thy commandments" (Ps. 119:30–31, 59–60)? Are you, like the Saviour, anxious to *fulfill the Scriptures*? O may writer and reader seek grace to pray from the heart, "Make me to go in the path of thy commandments; for therein do I delight. Incline my heart unto thy testimonies . . . Order my steps in thy word: and let not any iniquity have dominion over me" (Ps. 119:35–36, 133).

"I thirst."

100

4. Here we see the Saviour's submission to the Father's will.

The Saviour thirsted, and He who thirsted thus, remember, possessed all power in heaven and earth. Had He chosen to exercise His omnipotency, He could have readily satisfied His need. He that of old had caused the water to flow from the smitten rock for the refreshment of Israel in the wilderness had the same infinite resources at His disposal now. He who turned the water into wine at a word could have spoken the word of power here and met His own need. But He never once performed a miracle for His own benefit or comfort. When tempted by Satan to do this, He refused. Why did He now decline to satisfy His pressing need? Why hang there on the Cross with parched lips? Because in the volume of the Book that expressed God's will, it was written that He *should* thirst, and that thirsting He should be given vinegar to drink. And He came here to do God's will, and therefore did He submit.

In death, as in life, Scripture was for the Lord Jesus the authoritative Word of the living God. In the temptation He had refused to minister to His need apart from that Word by which He lived, and so now He makes known His need, not that it might be ministered unto but *that Scripture might be fulfilled.* Mark He does not Himself fulfill it—God can be trusted to take care of that—but He gives utterance to His distress so as to provide occasion for the fulfillment. As another has said, "The terrible thirst of crucifixion is upon Him, but that is not enough to force those parched lips to speak; but it is written; 'In my thirst they gave me vinegar to drink'—this opens them" (F. W. Grant). Here then, as ever, he shows Himself in active obedience to the will of God, which He came to accomplish. He simply says, "I thirst"; the vinegar is tendered, and the prophecy is fulfilled. What perfect absorption in His Father's will!

Again we pause to point an application to ourselves—a double one. First, the Lord Jesus delighted in the Father's will even when it involved the suffering of thirst. Are we so resigned to Him? Have we sought grace to say, "Not my will but Thine be done?" Can we exclaim, "Even so, Father, for so it seemed good in Thy sight?" Have we *learned* in whatever state we are in "therewith to be content" (Phil. 4:11)? But now mark a contrast. The Son of God was denied a draught of cold water to relieve His suffering—how different with us! God has given us a variety of refreshments to relieve us, yet how often are we unthankful! We have better things than a cup of water to delight us when thirsty, yet are we not grateful. O if this cry of Christ's were but believingly considered, it would make us bless God for what we now almost despise and beget contentment in us for the most common mercies. Did the Lord of Glory cry "I thirst" and have nothing in His extremity to comfort Him, and dost thou, who hast a thousand times forfeited all right to temporal as well as spiritual mercies, slight the common bounties of Providence! What! grumble at a cup of water, who deservest but a cup of wrath. O lay it to heart and learn to be content with what you have, though it be but the very barest necessaries of life. Complain not if you dwell in but a humble hovel, for your Saviour had not where to lay His head! Complain not if you have nought but bread to eat, for your Saviour lacked that for forty days! Complain not if you have only water to drink, for your Saviour was denied even that in the hour of death!

"I thirst."

5. Here we see how Christ can sympathize with His suffering people.

The problem of suffering has ever been a perplexing one. Why should suffering be necessary in a world that is governed by a perfect God?—a God who not only has the power to prevent evil but who *is* Love. Why should there be pain and wretchedness, sickness and death? As we look out on the world and take cognizance of its countless sufferers, we are bewildered. This world is but a Vale of Tears. A thin veneer of gaiety scarcely succeeds in hiding the drab facts of life. Philosophizing about the problem of suffering brings scant relief. After all our reasonings, we ask, Does God see? Is there knowledge with the Most High? Does He really care? Like all questions, these must be taken to the Cross. While they do not find there a complete answer, nevertheless they *do* meet that which satisfies the anxious heart. While the problem of suffering is not fully solved there, yet the Cross *does* throw sufficient light upon it to relieve the tension. The Cross shows us that God is not ignorant of our sorrows, for in the person of His Son He has Himself "borne our griefs, and carried our sorrows" (Isa. 53:4). The Cross shows us God is not unmindful of our distress and anguish, for becoming incarnate, *He suffered Himself*! The Cross tells us God is not indifferent to pain, for in the Saviour He *experienced* it!

What, then, is the value of these facts? This: "For we have not an high priest which cannot be touched with the feeling of our infirmities; but was in all points tempted [or tried] *like as we are*, yet without sin" (Heb. 4:15, emphasis added). Our Redeemer is not one so removed from us that He is unable to enter, sympathetically, into our sorrows, for He was Himself the "Man of Sorrows." Here, then, is comfort for the aching heart. No matter how despondent you may be, no matter how rugged your path and sad your lot, you are invited to spread it all before the Lord Jesus and cast all your care upon Him, knowing that "he careth for you" (1 Pet. 5:7). Is your body wracked with pain? So was His! Are you misunderstood, misjudged, misrepresented? So was He! Have those who are nearest and dearest turned away from you? They did from Him! Are you in the darkness? So was He for three hours! "Wherefore in all things it behooved him to be made like unto his brethren, that he might be a merciful and faithful high priest" (Heb. 2:17).

"I thirst."

6. Here we see the expression of a universal need.

Whether he articulates it or not, the natural man the world over is crying, "I thirst." Why this consuming desire to acquire

103

wealth? Why this craving for the honors and plaudits of the world? Why this mad rush after pleasure, the turning from one form of it to another with persistent and unwearied diligence? Why this eager search for wisdom—this scientific inquiry, this pursuit of philosophy, this ransacking of the writings of the ancients, and this ceaseless experimentation by the moderns? Why the insane craze for that which is novel? Why? Because there is an aching void in the soul. Because there is something remaining in every natural man that is *unsatisfied*. This is true of the millionaire equally as much as the pauper: the riches of the former bring no real contentment. It is as true of the globe-trotter equally as much as of the country rustic who has never been outside the bounds of his native country: traveling from one end of the earth to the other and back again, he fails to discover the secret of peace. Over all the cisterns of this world's providing is written in letters of ineffaceable truth, "Whosoever drinketh of this water *shall thirst again*" (John 4:13, emphasis added). So it is also with the religious man or woman: we mean, the religious *without Christ*. How many there are who go the weary round of religious performance and find nothing to meet their deep need! They are members of an evangelical denomination, they attend church regularly, contribute of their means to the pastor's support, read their Bibles occasionally, and sometimes pray, or if they use a "prayer book," *say* their prayers every night. And yet, after it all, if they are honest, their cry is still "I thirst."

The thirst is a *spiritual* one: that is why natural things cannot quench it. Unknown to themselves, their souls "thirsteth for God" (Ps. 42:2). God made us, and He alone can satisfy us. Said the Lord Jesus, "Whosoever drinketh of the water *that I shall give him* shall never thirst" (John 4:14, emphasis added). Christ alone can quench our thirst. He alone can meet the deep need of our hearts. He alone can impart that peace that the world knows nothing of and can neither bestow nor take away. O reader, once more I would address myself to your conscience. How is it with thee? Have you found that everything under the sun is only vanity and vexation of spirit? Have you discovered that the things of earth are unable to satisfy your *heart*? Is your soul cry "I thirst"? Then, is it not good news to hear there is One who *can* satisfy you? One we say, not a creed, not a form of religion, but a *person*—a living, divine person. He it is who says, "Come unto me, all ye that labour and are heavy laden, and I will give you rest" (Matt. 11:28). Heed, then, that sweet invitation. Come to Him now, just as you are. Come in faith, believing He will receive you; and then shall you sing

> I came to Jesus as I was,
> Weary, and worn, and sad;
> I found in Him a resting place,
> And He has made me glad.

O come to Christ. Delay not. You *are* "thirsty." Then you are the one He is seeking for—"Blessed are they which do hunger and thirst after righteousness: for they shall be filled" (Matt. 5:6).

Unsaved reader, reject not the Saviour, for if you die in your sins, your eternal cry will be "I thirst"! This is the moan of the damned. In the Lake of Fire the lost suffer amid the flames of God's wrath forever and ever. If Christ cried "I thirst" when He suffered the wrath of God for but three hours, what is the state of those who have to endure it for all eternity! When millions of years have gone, ten million more lie ahead. There is an everlasting thirst in hell that admits of no relief. Remember the awful words of the rich man: "And he cried and said, Father Abraham, have mercy on me, and send Lazarus, that he may dip the tip of his finger in water, and cool my tongue; *for I am tormented in this flame*" (Luke 16:24, emphasis added). O think, my reader. If physical thirst in the extreme is insufferable even now when endured but a few short hours, what will that thirst be that is infinitely beyond any present thirst, and that shall never be quenched! Say not it is cruel of God to deal thus with His erring creatures. Remember to what He exposed His own dear Son when sin was imputed to Him—surely the one who despises Christ is deserving of the hottest place in hell! Again we say, *Receive Him now as yours.* Receive Him as your Saviour, and submit to Him as your Lord.

"I thirst."

7. Here we see the enunication of an abiding principle.

There is a sense, a real one, in which *Christ still thirsts.* He is thirsting for the love and devotion of His own. He is yearning for *fellowship* with His blood-bought people. Here is one of the great marvels of grace—a redeemed sinner can offer that which satisfies the heart of Christ! I can understand how I ought to appreciate His love, but how wonderful that He—the all-sufficient One—should appreciate my love! I have learned how blessed to my own soul is communion with Him, but who would have supposed that my communion *was blessed to Christ*! Yet it is. For *this* He still "thirsts." Grace enables us to offer that which refreshes Him. Wondrous thought!

Have you ever noticed in John 4 that though Christ said to the woman who came to the well, "Give me to drink"—for He sat there "wearied" from the journey and heat—that He never took a drink of *water*? In the salvation and faith of that Samaritan woman, He found that which *refreshed His heart*! Love is never satisfied till there is a response and love in return! So with Christ. Here is the key to Revelation 3:20—"Behold, I stand at the door, and knock: if any man hear my voice, and open the door, I will come in to him, and will sup with him, and he with me." This is often applied to the unsaved, but its primary reference is to the Church. It pictures Christ seeking *the fellowship* of His own. He speaks of "supping," and in Scripture, supping is ever symbolic of communion, just as the Lord's Supper is a special season of communion between the Saviour and the saved. And observe in this passage Christ speaks of a *double* supping—"I will come in to him, and will sup with him, *and* he with me." Not only is it our unspeakable privilege to sup with Him, and to commune with Him, to delight ourselves in Him, but *He* "sups" with us. He finds in *our* communion something for *His* heart to feed upon, something that *refreshes* Him, and that something is our devotion and love. Yes, the Christ of God still "thirsts," thirsts for the affection of His own. O will you not offer that which will satisfy *Him*? Respond, then, to His own call—"Set me as a seal upon thine heart" (Song of Sol. 8:6).

6

The Word of Victory

When Jesus therefore had received the vinegar, he said, It is finished.

John 19:30

Our last two studies have been occupied with the tragedy of the Cross; we turn now to its *Triumph*. In His words, "My God, my God, why hast thou forsaken me?" we heard the Saviour's cry of *desolation*; in His words "I thirst" we listened to His cry of *lamentation*; now there falls upon our ears His cry of *jubilation*—"It is finished." From the words of the victim, we turn now to the words of the victor. It is proverbial that every cloud has its silver lining; so had the darkest cloud of all. The Cross of Christ has two great sides to it: it showed the profound depths of His humiliation, but it also marked the goal of the incarnation, and further, it told of the consummation of His mission, and it forms the basis of our salvation.

"It is finished." The ancient Greeks boasted of being able to say much in little—"to give a sea of matter in a drop of language" was regarded as the perfection of oratory. What they sought is here found. "It is finished" is but one word in the original, yet in that word is wrapped up the Gospel of God; in that word is contained the ground of the believer's assurance; in that word is discovered the sum of all joy and the very spirit of all divine consolation.

"It is finished." This was not the despairing cry of a helpless martyr; it was not an expression of satisfaction that the termination of His sufferings was now reached; it was not the last gasp of a worn-out life. No, rather was it the declaration on the part of the divine Redeemer that all for which He came from heaven to earth to do was now done; that all that was needed to reveal the full character of God had now been accomplished; that all that was required by the law before sinners could be saved had now been performed: that the full price of our redemption was now paid.

"It is finished." The great purpose of God in the history of man was now accomplished—accomplished *de jure* as it will yet be *de facto*. From the beginning, God's purpose has always been one and indivisible. It had been declared to men in various ways: in symbol and type, by mysterious hints and by plain intimations, through Messianic prediction and through didactic declaration. That purpose of God may be summarized thus: to display His grace and to magnify His Son in the creating of children in His own image and glory. And at the Cross the foundation was laid that was to make this possible and actual.

"It is finished." *What* was finished? The answer to this question is a very full one, though a number of excellent expositors have sought to limit the scope of these words and to confine them strictly to a single application. We are told it was *the prophecies* concerning the sufferings of the Saviour that were finished, and that He referred *only* to this. It is readily granted that the immediate reference *was* to the Messianic predictions, yet we think there are good and sufficient reasons for *not confining* our Lord's words here to them. Yea, to us it seems certain that Christ referred specially to His sacrificial work, for *all* Scripture concerning His suffering and shame was *not yet* fulfilled. There still remained the dismissal of His Spirit into the hands of the Father (Ps. 31:5); there still remained the "piercing" with the spear (Zech. 12:10; and note that the word used for the piercing of His hands and feet—the *act* of crucifixion—in Ps. 22:16 is a different one); there still remained the preserving of His bones unbroken (Ps. 34:20) and the burial in the rich man's grave (Isa. 53:9).

"It is finished." *What* was finished? We answer: His sacrificial work. It is true there yet remained the act of death itself, which was necessary for the making of atonement. But as is so often the case here in John's Gospel—wherein our text is found—(cf. John 12:23, 31; 13:31; 16:5; 17:4), the Lord here speaks *anticipatively* of the completion of His work. Moreover, it must be remembered that the three hours of darkness was already past, the awful cup had already been drained, His precious blood had already been shed, the outpoured wrath of God had already been endured; and these are the primary elements in the making of propitiation. The sacrificial work of the Saviour, then, was completed, excepting only the act of death, which followed immediately. But, as we shall see, the completing of the sacrificial work made an end of a number of things, and to them we shall now turn our attention.

"It is finished."

1. Here we see the accomplished fulfillment of all the prophecies that had been written of Him ere He should die.

This is the immediate thought of the context: "When Jesus therefore had received the vinegar, he said, It is finished" (John 19:30). Centuries beforehand, the prophets of God had described step by step the humiliation and suffering that the coming Saviour should undergo. One by one these had been fulfilled, wonderfully fulfilled, fulfilled to the very letter. Had prophecy declared that He should be the *woman's* seed? (Gen.

111

3:15), then He *was* "made of a woman" (Gal. 4:4). Had prophecy announced that His mother should be a "virgin"? (Isa. 7:14), then was it literally fulfilled (Matt. 1:18). Had prophecy revealed that He should be of the seed of Abraham? (Gen. 22:18), then mark its fulfillment (Matt. 1:1). Had prophecy made it known that He should be a lineal descendant of David? (2 Sam. 7:12–13), then such He actually was (Rom. 1:3). Had prophecy said that He should be named *before* He was born? (Isa. 49:1), then so it came to pass (Luke 1:31). Had prophecy foretold that He should be born in Bethlehem of Judea? (Mic. 5:2), then mark how this very village was actually His birthplace. Had prophecy forewarned that His birth should entail sorrowing for others? (Jer. 31:15), then behold its tragic fulfillment (Matt. 2:16–18). Had prophecy foreshown that the Messiah should appear before the scepter of tribal ascendancy had departed from Judah? (Gen. 49:10), then so He did, for though the ten tribes were in captivity, Judah was still in the land at the time of His advent. Had prophecy referred to the flight into Egypt and the subsequent return into Palestine? (Hosea 11:1; cf. Isa. 49:3, 6), then so it came to pass (Matt. 2:14–15).

Had prophecy made mention of one going before Christ to make ready His way? (Mal. 3:1), then see its fulfillment in the person of John the Baptist. Had prophecy made it known that at the Messiah's appearing that "then the eyes of the blind shall be opened, and the ears of the deaf shall be unstopped. Then shall the lame man leap as an hart, and the tongue of the dumb sing"? (Isa. 35:5–6), then read through the four Gospels and see how blessedly this proved true. Had prophecy spoken of Him as "poor and needy"? (Ps. 40:17—see beginning of the psalm), then behold Him not having where to lay His head. Had prophecy intimated that He should speak in parables? (Ps. 78:2), then such was frequently His method of teaching. Had prophecy depicted Him stilling the tempest? (Ps. 107:29), then this is exactly what He did. Had prophecy heralded His triumphal entry into Jerusalem? (Zech. 9:9), then so it came to pass.

Had prophecy announced that His person should be despised? (Isa. 53:3), that He should be rejected by the Jews? (Isa. 8:14), that He should be hated "without a cause"? (Ps. 69:4), then sad to say, such was precisely the case. Had prophecy painted the whole picture of His degradation and crucifixion? then was it vividly reproduced. There had been the betrayal by a familiar friend, the forsaking by His cherished disciples, the being led to the slaughter, the being taken to judgment, the appearing of false witnesses against Him, the refusal on His part to make defense, the establishing of His innocency, the unjust condemnation, the sentence of capital punishment passed upon Him, the literal piercing of His hands and feet, the being numbered with transgressors, the mockery of the crowd, the casting lots for His garments—all predicted centuries beforehand, and all fulfilled to the very letter. The last prophecy of all that remained, ere He committed His Spirit into the hands of His Father, had now been fulfilled. He cried, "I thirst," and after the tendering of the vinegar and gall, *all* was now "accomplished"; and as the Lord Jesus reviewed the entire scope of the prophetic Word *and saw its full realization*, He cried, "It is finished!"

It only remains for us to point out that as there was a complete set of prophecies that had to do with the *first* advent of the Saviour, so also is there a complete set of prophecies that have to do with His *second* advent—the latter as definite, as personal, and as comprehensive in their scope as the former. As, then, we see the actual fulfillment of those that had to do with His first coming to the earth, we may look forward with absolute confidence and assurance to the fulfillment of those that have to do with His second coming. And, as we have seen that the former set of prophecies were fulfilled *literally*, actually, personally, so also must we expect the latter set to be. To grant the literal fulfillment of the former, and then to seek to spiritualize and symbolize the latter, is not only grossly inconsistent and illogical but is highly injurious to us and deeply dishonoring to God and to His Word.

"It is finished."

2. Here we see the completion of His sufferings.

But what tongue or pen can describe the sufferings of the Saviour? O the unutterable anguish—physical, mental, and spiritual—that He endured! Appropriately was He designated "The Man of Sorrows": sufferings at the hands of men, at the hands of Satan, and at the hands of God; pain inflicted upon Him by enemies and friends alike. From the beginning He walked amid the shadows that the Cross cast athwart His path. Hear His lament: "I am afflicted and ready to die *from my youth up*" (Ps. 88:15, emphasis added). What a light this throws on His earlier years! Who can say how much is contained in those words? For us, an impenetrable veil is cast over the future; none of us know what a day may bring forth. But the Saviour knew the end from the beginning! One has only to read through the Gospels to learn how the awful Cross was ever before Him. At the marriage feast of Cana, where all was gladness and merriment, He makes solemn reference to "his hour" not yet come. When Nicodemus interviewed Him at night, the Saviour referred to the "lifting up of the Son of Man." When James and John came to request from Him the two places of honor in His coming kingdom, He made mention of the "cup" that He had to drink and of the "baptism" wherewith He must be baptized. When Peter confessed that He was the Christ, the Son of the living God, He turned to His disciples and began to show unto them "how that he must go unto Jerusalem, and suffer many things of the elders and chief priests and scribes, and be killed, and be raised again the third day" (Matt. 16:21). When Moses and Elijah stood with Him on the Mount of Transfiguration, it was to speak of "his decease which he should accomplish at Jerusalem" (Luke 9:31).

If it is true we are quite unable to estimate the sufferings of Christ due to the *anticipation* of the Cross, still less can we fathom the dread reality itself. The physical sufferings were excruciating, but even this was as nothing compared with His anguish of soul. To a consideration of these sufferings we have already devoted several paragraphs in previous chapters, yet we make no apology in turning to them again. We cannot contemplate too often what the Saviour endured in order to secure our salvation. The better we are acquainted with His sufferings, and the more frequently we meditate thereon, the warmer will be our love and the deeper our gratitude.

At last the closing hours have come. There had been the terrible experience in Gethsemane followed by the appearings before Caiaphas, before Pilate, before Herod, and back again before Pilate. There had been the scourging and mocking by the brutal soldiers, the journey to Calvary, the fastening of His hands and feet to the cruel Tree. There had been the reviling of the priests, the crowd, and the two thieves crucified with Him. There had been the callous indifference of a vulgar mob, among whom none took pity and none spoke a word of comfort (Ps. 69:20). There had been the awful cloud that hid the Father's face, which wrung from Him the bitter cry, "My God, my God, why hast thou forsaken me?" There had been the parched lips that drew from Him the exclamation "I thirst." There had been the fearful conflict with the power of darkness as the serpent "bruised" His heel. Well might the sufferer ask, "Is it nothing to you, all ye that pass by? behold, *and see if there be any sorrow like unto my sorrow*, which is done unto me, wherewith the LORD hath afflicted me in the day of his fierce anger" (Lam. 1:12, emphasis added).

But now the suffering is ended. That from which His holy soul shrank is over. The Lord has bruised Him; man and devil have done their worst. The cup has been drained. The awful storm of God's wrath has spent itself. The darkness is ended. The sword of divine justice is sheathed. The wages of sin have been paid. The prophecies of His sufferings are all fulfilled. The

Cross has been "endured." Divine holiness has been fully satisfied. With a cry of triumph—a *loud* cry, a cry that reverberated throughout the entire universe—the Saviour exclaims, "It is finished." The ignominy and shame, the suffering and agony, are past. Never again shall He experience pain. Never again shall He endure the contradiction of sinners against Himself. Never again shall He be in the hands of Satan. Never again shall the light of God's countenance be hidden from Him. Blessed be God, all that is *finished*!

> The head that once was crowned with thorns is crowned
> with glory now;
> A royal diadem adorns the mighty Victor's brow.
> The highest place that Heaven affords is His by Sovereign
> right,
> The King of kings and Lord of lords, and Heaven's eternal
> Light.
> The Joy of all who dwell above, the Joy of all below,
> To whom He manifests His love, and Grants His name to
> know.

"It is finished."

3. Here we see the goal of the incarnation is reached.

Scripture indicates there is a special work peculiar to each of the divine persons, though, like the persons themselves, it is not always easy to distinguish between their respective works. God the Father is specially concerned in the government of the world. He ruleth over all the works of His hands. God the Son is specially concerned in the work of Redemption: He was the One who came here to die for sinners. God the Spirit is specially concerned with the Scriptures: He was the One who moved holy men of old to speak the messages of God, as He is the One who now gives spiritual illumination and understanding and guides into the truth. But it is with the work of God the Son we are here particularly concerned.

Before the Lord Jesus came to this earth, a definite work was committed to Him. In the volume of the book it was written of Him, and He came to do the recorded will of God. Even as a boy of twelve, the "Father's business" was before His heart and occupied His attention. Again, in John 5:36 we find Him saying, "But I have greater witness than that of John: *for the works which the Father hath given me to finish, the same works that I do*" (emphasis added). And on the last night before His death, in that wonderful high priestly prayer, we find Him saying, "I have glorified thee on the earth: *I have finished the work which thou gavest me to do*" (John 17:4, emphasis added).

In his book *The Seven Sayings of Christ on the Cross*, Dr. Anderson-Berry makes use of an illustration from history that by its striking antithesis shows up the meaning and glory of the finished work of Christ. Elizabeth, Queen of England, the idol of society and the leader of European fashion, when on her deathbed turned to her lady in waiting, and said: "O my God! It is over. I have come to the end of it—the end, the end. To have only one life, and to have done with it! To have lived, and loved, and triumphed; and now to know it is over! One may defy everything else but this." And as the listener sat watching, in a few moments more the face whose slightest smile had brought her courtiers to their feet turned into a mask of lifeless clay and returned the anxious gaze of her servant with nothing more than a vacant stare. Such was the end of one whose meteoric course had been the envy of half the world. It could not be said that she had "finished" anything, for with her all was "vanity and vexation of spirit." How different with the end of the Saviour!—"I have glorified thee on the earth: I have *finished* the work which thou gavest me to do."

The mission upon which God had sent His Son into the world was now accomplished. It was not actually finished till He breathed His last, but death was only an instant ahead. And in anticipation of it He cries, "It is finished." The difficult work is done. The divinely given task is performed. A work more honorable and momentous than ever entrusted to man or angels has been completed. That for which He had left heaven's glory, that for which He had taken upon Him the form of a servant, and that for which He had remained upon earth for thirty-three years to do was now consummated. Nothing remained to be added. The goal of the incarnation is reached. With what joyous triumph must He here have viewed the arduous and costly work that committed to Him had now been perfected!

"It is finished." The mission upon which God had sent His Son into the world was accomplished. That which had been eternally purposed had come to pass. The plan of God had been fully carried out. It is true that the Saviour had been by "wicked hands . . . crucified and slain," yet was He "delivered by the determinate counsel and foreknowledge of God" (Acts 2:23). It is true that the kings of the earth stood up, and the rulers were gathered together against the Lord and against His Christ; nevertheless it was but for to do what God's hand and God's counsel "determined before to be done" (Acts 4:28). Because He is the Most High, God's secret will *cannot* be thwarted. Because He is supreme, God's counsel *must* stand. Because He is Almighty, God's purpose *cannot* be overthrown. Again and again the Scriptures insist upon the *irresistibility* of the pleasure of the Lord God. Because this truth is now so generally called into question, we subjoin seven passages that affirm it: "But he is in one mind, and who can turn him? and what his soul desireth, *even that he doeth*" (Job 23:13, emphasis added). "I know that thou canst do every thing, *and that no thought can be witholden from thee*" (Job 42:2, emphasis added). "But our God is in the heavens: *he hath done whatsoever he hath pleased*" (Ps. 115:3, emphasis added). "There is no wisdom nor understanding nor counsel against the LORD" (Prov. 21:30). "For the LORD of hosts hath purposed, and who shall disannul it? and his hand is stretched out, and who shall turn it back?" (Isa. 14:27). "Remember the former things of old: for I am God, and there is none else; I am God, and there is none like me. Declaring

118

the end from the beginning, and from ancient times the things that are not yet done, saying, My counsel shall stand, and I will do all my pleasure" (Isa. 46:9–10). "And all the inhabitants of the earth are reputed as nothing: and he doeth according to *his will* in the army of heaven, *and* among the inhabitants of the earth: and *none can stay his hand*, or say unto him, What doest thou?" (Dan. 4:35, emphasis added). And in the triumphant cry of the Saviour—"It is finished"—we have a prophecy and pledge of the *ultimate* carrying out of God's plan *completely and irresistibly*. At the end of time, when everything is wound up, and God's purpose has been fully consummated, when everything has been done that He before determined should be done, then shall it be said again, "It is finished."*

"It is finished."

4. Here we see the accomplishment of the atonement.

Above we have spoken of Christ reaching the goal of the incarnation, and of the consummation of His mission to the earth; what that goal and mission was the Scriptures plainly reveal. The Son of Man came here "to seek and to save that which was lost" (Luke 19:10). Christ Jesus came into the world "to save sinners" (1 Tim. 1:15). God sent forth His Son, born of a woman, "to redeem them that were under the law" (Gal. 4:5). He was manifested "to take away our sins" (1 John 3:5). And all this involved the Cross. The "lost" that He came to seek could only be found there—in the place of death and under the condemnation of God. Sinners could be "saved" only by one taking their place and bearing their iniquities. They who were under the law could be "redeemed" only by another fulfilling its requirements and suffering its curse. Our sins could be "taken away" only by their being blotted out by the precious blood of Christ. The demands of justice *must*

*For a fuller discussion of this important subject, see the author's book *The Sovereignty of God*.

be met; the requirements of God's holiness *must* be satisfied; the awful debt we incurred *must* be paid. And on the Cross this was done—done by none less than the Son of God, done perfectly, done once for all.

"It is finished." That to which so many types looked forward, that which so much in the tabernacle and its ritual foreshadowed, that of which so many of God's prophets had spoken, was now accomplished. A *covering* from sin and its shame—typified by the coats of skin with which the Lord God clothed our first parents—was now provided. The *more excellent sacrifice*—typified by Abel's lamb—had now been offered. A *shelter* from the storm of divine judgment—typified by the ark of Noah—was now furnished. The *only begotten and well-beloved Son*—typified by Abraham's offering up of Isaac—had already been placed upon the altar. A *protection* from the avenging angel—typified by the shed blood of the Passover lamb—was now supplied. A *cure* from the serpent's bite—typified by the serpent of brass upon the pole—was now made ready for sinners. The providing of a *life-giving fountain*—typified by Moses striking the rock—was now effected.

"It is finished." The Greek word here, *teleo*, is variously translated in the New Testament. A glance at some of the different renderings in other passages will enable us to discern the fullness and finality of the term used by the Saviour. In Matthew 11:1 *teleo* is rendered as follows, "When Jesus had made an end of commanding his twelve disciples, he departed thence." In Matthew 17:24 it is rendered, "They that received tribute money came to Peter, and said, Doth not your master pay tribute?" In Luke 2:39 it is rendered, "And when they had performed all things according to the law of the Lord, they returned into Galilee." In Luke 18:31 it is rendered, "All things that are written by the prophets concerning the Son of man shall be accomplished." Putting these together, we learn the scope of the Saviour's sixth cross utterance. "It is finished." He cried: it is "made an end of"; it is "paid"; it is "performed"; it is "accomplished." What was made an end of?—our sins and their guilt. What was "paid"?—the price of our redemption. What was "performed"?—the utmost requirements of the law. What was "accomplished"?—the work that the Father had given Him to do. What was "finished"?—the making of atonement.

God has furnished at least four *proofs* that Christ *did* finish the work that was given Him to do. First, in the rending of the veil, which showed that the way to God was now open. Second, in the raising of Christ from the dead, which evidenced God had accepted His sacrifice. Third, the exaltation of Christ to His own right hand, which demonstrated the value of Christ's work and the Father's delight in His person. Fourth, the sending to earth of the Holy Spirit to apply the virtues and benefits of Christ's atoning death.

"It is finished." What was "finished"? The work of atonement. What is the value of that to us? This: to the sinner, it is a message of glad tidings. All that a holy God requires has been done. Nothing is left for the sinner to add. No works from us are demanded as the price of our salvation. All that is necessary for the sinner is to rest now by faith upon what Christ did. "The gift of God is eternal life through Jesus Christ our Lord" (Rom. 6:23). To the believer, the knowledge that the atoning work of Christ is finished brings a sweet relief over against all the defects and imperfections of his services. There is nothing "finished" that we do; all our duties are imperfect. There is much of sin and vanity in the very best of our efforts, but the grand relief is that we are "*complete*" in Christ (Col. 2:10)! Christ and His finished work is the ground of all our hopes.

> Upon a Life I did not live,
> Upon a Death I did not die,
> Another's death—Another's life
> I cast my soul eternally.
> Bold shall I stand in that great day,
> For who aught to my charge can lay?
> Fully absolved by Christ I am,
> From sin's tremendous curse and blame.

"It is finished."

5. Here we see the end of our sins.

The sins of the believer—all of them—were transferred to the Saviour. As saith the Scripture, "The LORD *hath laid on him* the iniquity of us all" (Isa. 53:6, emphasis added). If, then, God laid my iniquities on Christ, they are no longer on me. Sin there is *in* me, for the old Adamic nature remains in the believer till death or till Christ's return, should He come before I die; but there is no sin *on* me. This distinction between sin *in* and sin *on* is a vital one, and there should be little difficulty in apprehending it. Were I to say the judge passed sentence *on* a criminal, and that he is now *under* sentence of death, everyone would understand what I meant. In like manner, everyone out of Christ has the sentence of God's condemnation resting *upon* him. But when a sinner believes in the Lord Jesus, receives Him as his Lord and Master, he is no longer "under condemnation"—sin is no longer *on him*, that is, the *guilt*, the *condemnation*, the *penalty* of sin is no longer upon him. And why? Because Christ bore our sins in His own body on the Tree (1 Pet. 2:24)—the guilt, condemnation, and penalty of our sins was *transferred to our substitute*. Hence, because my sins were transferred to Christ, they are no more upon me.

This precious truth was strikingly illustrated in Old Testament times in connection with Israel's annual Day of Atonement. On that day, Aaron, the high priest (type of Christ), made satisfaction to God for the sins that Israel had committed during the previous year. The manner in which this was done is described in Leviticus 16. Two goats were taken and presented before the Lord at the door of the tabernacle: this was *before* anything was done with them; it represented Christ presenting Himself to God, offering to come into this world and be the Saviour of sinners. One of the goats was then taken and *killed*, and its blood was carried into the tabernacle, within the veil, into the Holy of Holies, and there it was sprinkled before and upon the mercy seat—foreshadowing Christ offering Himself as a sacrifice *to God*, to meet the demands of His justice and satisfy the requirements of His holiness. Then we read that Aaron came out of the tabernacle and laid both his hands upon the head of the second (living) goat—signifying an act of *identification* by which Aaron is the representative of the whole nation, identifying the people with it, acknowledging that *its* doom was what *their* sins merited, and that, today, corresponds with the hands of faith laying hold of Christ and identifying ourselves with Him in His death. Having laid his hands on the head of the live goat, Aaron now *confessed* over him "*all* the iniquities of the children of Israel, and *all* their transgressions in *all* their sins, *putting them upon* the head of the goat" (Lev. 16:21, emphasis added). Thus were Israel's sins *trans*ferred to their substitute. Finally, we are told, "And the goat shall *bear upon him* all their iniquities unto a land *not inhabited*: and he shall let go the goat in the wilderness" (Lev. 16:22, emphasis added). The goat bearing Israel's sins was taken unto an uninhabited wilderness, and the people of God saw him and their sins *no more*! In type this was Christ taking our sins into that desolate land *where God was not*, and there making an end of them. The Cross of Christ, then, is *the grave* of our sins!

"It is finished."

6. Here we see the fulfillment of the law's requirements.

"The law is holy, and the commandment holy, and just, and good" (Rom. 7:12). How could it be anything less when Jehovah Himself had framed and given it! The fault lay not in the law but in man who, being depraved and sinful, could not keep it. Yet that law must be kept, and kept by a man, so that the law might be honored and magnified, and its giver vindicated. Therefore we read, "For what the law could not do, in that it was weak through the flesh, God sending his own Son in the likeness of sinful flesh, and for sin, condemned sin in the flesh: that the righteousness of the law might be fulfilled in [not by] us, who walk not after flesh, but after the Spirit" (Rom. 8:3–4).

123

The "weakness" here is that of fallen man. The sending forth of God's Son in the likeness of sin's flesh (Greek) refers to the incarnation, as we read in another Scripture: "God sent forth his Son, born of woman, born under the law, to redeem those who were under the law" (Gal. 4:4–5 RSV). Yes, the Saviour was born "under the law," born under it that He might keep it perfectly in thought, word, and deed. "Think not that I am come to destroy the law, or the prophets: I am not come to destroy, but to fulfil" (Matt. 5:17); such was His claim.

But not only did the Saviour *keep* the precepts of the law; He also suffered its penalty and endured its curse. We had broken it, and taking our place, He must receive its just sentence. Having received its penalty and endured its curse, the demands of the law are fully met and justice is satisfied. Therefore is it written of believers, "*Christ* hath redeemed us from the curse of the law, being made a curse for us" (Gal. 3:13). And again, "For Christ is the end of the law for righteousness to every one that believeth" (Rom. 10:4). And yet again, "For ye are not under the law, but under grace" (Rom. 6:14).

> Free from the Law, O happy condition!
> Jesus hath bled, and there is remission,
> Cursed by the law and dead by the fall,
> Grace hath redeemed us once for all.

"It is finished."

7. Here we see the destruction of Satan's power.

See it by faith. The Cross sounded the death knell of the devil's power. To human appearances it looked like the moment of his greatest triumph, yet in reality, it was the hour of his ultimate defeat. In view of the Cross (see context) the Saviour declared, "Now is the judgment of this world: now shall the prince of this world be cast out" (John 12:31). It is true that Satan has not yet been chained and cast into the bottomless pit, nevertheless, sentence has been passed (though not yet executed); his doom is certain, and his power is already broken so far as believers are concerned.

For the Christian the devil is a *vanquished* foe. He was defeated by Christ at the Cross—"that through death he might destroy him that had the power of death, that is, the devil" (Heb. 2:14). Believers have already been "delivered from the power of darkness" and translated into the kingdom of God's dear Son (Col. 1:13). Satan, then, should be treated as a *defeated* enemy. No longer has he any legitimate *claim* upon us. Once we were his lawful "captives," but Christ has freed us. Once we walked "according to the prince of the power of the air," but now we are to follow the example that Christ has left us. Once Satan "worked in us," but now *God* worketh in us both to will and to do of His good pleasure. All that we now have to do is to "resist the devil," and the promise is, "he will flee from you" (James 4:7).

"It is finished." Here was the triumphant answer to the rage of man and the enmity of Satan. It tells of the perfect work that meets sin in the place of judgment. All was *completed* just as God would have it, just as the prophets had foretold, just as the Old Testament ceremonial had foreshadowed, just as divine holiness demanded, and just as sinners needed. How strikingly appropriate in this sixth cross utterance of the Saviour found in John's Gospel—the Gospel that displays the glory of Christ's deity! He does not here commend His work to the approval of God but seals it with *His own imprimatur*, attesting it as complete, and giving it the all-sufficient sanction of *His own* approval. None other than the Son of God says, "IT IS finished"—who, then, dare doubt or question it.

"It is finished." Reader, do you believe it? Or are you trying to add something of our own to the finished work of Christ to secure the favor of God? All you have to do is to accept the pardon that He purchased. *God is satisfied* with the work of Christ, why are not you? Sinner, the moment you believe God's testimony concerning His beloved Son, that moment every sin you have committed is blotted out, and you stand accepted in Christ! O would you not like to possess the assurance that there is nothing between your soul and God? Would you not like to know that every sin had been atoned for and put away? Then believe *what God's Word says* about Christ's death. Rest not on your feelings and experiences but on the written Word. There is only one way of finding peace, and that is through faith in the shed blood of God's Lamb.

"It is finished." Do you *really* believe it? Or are you endeavoring to add something of your own to it and thus merit the favor of God? Some years ago a Christian farmer was deeply concerned over an unsaved carpenter. The farmer sought to set before his neighbor the Gospel of God's grace and to explain how the finished work of Christ was *sufficient* for his soul to rest upon. But the carpenter persisted in the belief that he must do something himself. One day the farmer asked the carpenter to make for him a gate, and when the gate was ready, he carried it away to his wagon. He arranged for the carpenter to call on him the next morning and see the gate as it hung in the field. At the appointed hour the carpenter arrived and was surprised to find the farmer standing by with a sharp axe in his hand. "What are you going to do?" he asked. "I am going to add a few cuts and strokes to your work" was the response. "But there is no need for it," replied the carpenter; "the gate is alright as it is. I did all that was necessary to it." The farmer took no notice, but lifting his axe, he slashed and hacked at the gate until it was completely spoiled. "Look what you have done!" cried the carpenter; "you have *ruined my work*!" "Yes," said the farmer, "and that is exactly what you are trying to do. You are seeking to nullify the finished work of Christ by your own miserable additions to it!" God used this forceful object lesson to show the carpenter his mistake, and he was led to cast himself by faith upon what Christ had done for sinners. Reader, will *you* do the same?

7

The Word of Contentment

And when Jesus had cried with a loud voice, he said,
Father, into thy hands I commend my spirit:
and having said thus, he gave up the ghost.

Luke 23:46

"And when Jesus had cried with a loud voice, he said, Father, into thy hands I commend my spirit: and having said thus, he gave up the ghost" (Luke 23:46). These words set before us *the last act* of the Saviour ere He expired. It was an act of contentment, of faith, of confidence, and of love. The person to whom He committed the precious treasure of His Spirit was His own Father. *Father* is an encouraging and assuring title: well may a son commit any concern, however dear, into the hands of a father, especially such a Son into the hands of such a Father. That which was committed into the hands of the Father was His "spirit," which was on the point of being separated from the body. Scripture reveals man as a tripartite being: "spirit and soul and body" (1 Thess. 5:23). There is a difference between the soul and the spirit, though it is not easy to predicate wherein they are dissimilar. The spirit appears to be *the highest part* of our complex being. It is that which, particularly, distinguishes man from the beasts and that which links him to God. The spirit is that which *God* formeth within us (Zech. 12:1); therefore is He called "the God of the spirits of all flesh" (Num. 16:22). At death the spirit *returns* to God who *gave* it (Eccles. 12:7). The act by which the Saviour placed His Spirit into the hands of the Father was an act of faith—"I commend." It was a blessed act designed as a precedent for all His people. The last point observable is *the manner* in which Christ performed this act; He uttered those words "with a loud voice." He spoke that all might hear, and that His enemies who judged Him destitute and forsaken of God might know it was not so any longer, but instead, that He was dear to His Father still, and could put His Spirit confidently into His Father's hands.

"Father, into thy hands I commend my spirit." This was the last utterance of the Saviour ere He expired. While He hung upon the Cross, seven times His lips moved in speech. Seven is the number of *completeness* or *perfection*. At Calvary, then, as everywhere, the perfections of the Blessed One were displayed. Seven is also the number of *rest* in a *finished* work: in six days God made heaven and earth, and in the seventh He rested, contemplating with satisfaction that which He had pronounced "very good." So here with Christ: a work had been given Him to do, and that work was now done. Just as the sixth day brought the work of creation and reconstruction to a completion, so the sixth utterance of the Saviour was "It is finished." And just as the seventh day was the day of rest and satisfaction, so the seventh utterance of the Saviour brings Him to the place of rest—the Father's hands.

Seven times the dying Saviour spoke. Three of His utterances concerned men: to one He gave the promise that the man should be with Him that day in paradise; to another He confided His mother; to the mass of spectators He made mention of His thirst. Three of His utterances were addressed to God: to the Father He prayed for His murderers; to God He uttered His mournful plaint; and now into the hands of the Father He commends His Spirit. In the hearing of God and men, angels and devil, He had cried in triumph, "It is finished."

"Father, into thy hands I commend my spirit." It is noteworthy that this closing cry of the Saviour had been uttered by the Spirit of prophecy long centuries before the incarnation. In the thirty-first Psalm we hear David saying, anticipatively, "In thee, O LORD, do I put my trust; let me never be ashamed: deliver me in thy righteousness. Bow down thine ear to me; deliver me speedily: be thou my strong rock, for an house of defence to save me. For thou art my rock and my fortress; therefore for thy name's sake lead me, and guide me. Pull me out of the net that they have laid privily for me: for thou art my strength. Into thine hand I commit my spirit: thou hast redeemed me, O LORD God of truth" (vv. 1–5).

In connection with each one of our Saviour's cross utterances, a prophecy was fulfilled. First, He cried, "Father, forgive them, for they know not what they do," and this fulfilled Isaiah 53:12—"made intercession for the transgressors." Second, He promised the thief, "Today shalt thou be with me in paradise," and this was a fulfillment of the prophecy of the angel to Joseph—"thou shalt call his name JESUS: for he shall save his people from their sins" (Matt. 1:21). Third, to His mother He said, "Woman, behold thy son," and this fulfilled the prophecy of Simeon—"A sword shall pierce through thy own soul also" (Luke 2:35). Fourth, He had asked, "My God, my God, why hast thou forsaken me?" and these were the identical words of Psalm 22:1. Fifth, He exclaimed, "I thirst," and this was in fulfillment of Psalm 69:21—"In my thirst they gave me vinegar to drink." Sixth, He shouted in triumph, "It is finished," and these are almost the very words with which that wonderful twenty-second Psalm concludes—"He hath *done*," or, as Hebrew might well be rendered, "*He hath finished*," the context showing what He *had* done, namely, the work of atonement. Finally, He prayed, "Father, into thy hands I commend my spirit," and, as we have shown above, He was but quoting as it had been written of Him beforehand in Psalm 31. O the *wonders* of the Cross! We shall never reach the end of them.

"Father, into thy hands I commend my spirit."

1. Here we see the Saviour back again in communion with the Father.

This is exceedingly precious. For a while that communion was broken—broken outwardly—as the light of God's holy countenance was hidden from the Sin Bearer, but now the darkness had passed and was ended forever. Up to the Cross there had been perfect and unbroken communion between the Father and the Son. It is exquisitely lovely to mark how the awful "cup" itself had been accepted from the Father's hand—"The cup which my Father hath given me, shall I not drink it?" (John 18:11). On the Cross, at the beginning, the Lord Jesus is still found in communion with the Father, for had He not cried, "*Father*, forgive them!" His *first* cross utterance, then, was "*Father* forgive," and now His *last* word is, "*Father*, into thy hands I commend my spirit." But *between* those utterances He had hung there for six hours: three spent in sufferings at the hand of man and Satan; three spent in suffering at the hand of God, as the sword of divine justice was "awakened" to smite Jehovah's fellow. During those last three hours, God had withdrawn from the Saviour, evoking that terrible cry, "My God, my God, why hast thou forsaken me?" But now all is done. The cup is drained, the storm of wrath has spent itself, the darkness is past, and the Saviour is seen once more in communion with the Father—never more to be broken.

"Father." How often this word was upon the Saviour's lips! His first recorded utterance was, "Wist ye not that I must be about *my Father's* business?" In what was probably His first formal discourse—the Sermon on the Mount—He speaks of the "Father" seventeen times. While in His final discourse to the disciples—the Pascal Discourse found in John 14–16—the word "Father" is found no less than forty-five times! In the next chapter, John 17, which contains what is known as Christ's great high priestly prayer, He speaks to and of the Father six times more. And now the last time He speaks ere He lays down His life, He says again, "Father, into thy hands I commend my spirit."

And how blessed it is that *His* Father is *our* Father! Ours because His. How wonderful this is! How unspeakably precious that I can look up to the great and living God and say, "Father," *my* Father! What comfort is contained in this title! What assurance it conveys! God is my Father, then He *loves* me, loves me *as* He loves Christ Himself (John 17:23). God is my Father and loves me, then He *careth* for me. God is my Father and careth for me, then He *will* supply *all* my need (Phil. 4:19). God is my Father, then He will see to it that no harm shall betide me, yea, that all things shall be made to work together for my *good*. O that His children entered more deeply and practically into the blessedness of this relationship, then would they joyfully exclaim with the apostle, "Behold, what manner of love the Father hath bestowed *upon us*, that *we* should be called *the sons of God*" (1 John 3:1, emphasis added)!

"Father, into thy hands I commend my spirit."

2. Here we see a designed contrast.

For more than twelve hours Christ had been in the hands of men. Of this had He spoken to His disciples when He forewarned them that "the Son of man shall be betrayed into the hands of men: and they shall kill him" (Matt. 17:22–23). Of this had He made mention amid the awful solemnities of Gethsemane—"Then cometh he to his disciples, and saith unto them, Sleep on now, and take your rest: behold, the hour is at hand, and the Son of man is betrayed into the hands of sinners" (Matt. 26:45). To this the angels had reference on the resurrection morning, saying to the woman, "He is not here, but is risen: remember how he spake unto you when he was yet in Galilee, saying, The Son of man must be delivered into the hands of sinful men, and be crucified, and the third day rise again" (Luke 24:6–7). This received its fulfillment when the Lord Jesus delivered Himself up to those who came to arrest Him in the garden. As we saw in an earlier chapter, Christ could have easily avoided arrest. All He had to do was to leave the officers of the priests prostrate on the ground and walk quietly away. But He did not do so. The appointed hour had struck. The time when He should submit Himself to be led as a lamb to the slaughter had arrived. And He delivered Himself into "the hands of sinners." How they treated Him is well known; they took full advantage of their opportunity. They gave full vent to the hatred of the carnal heart for God. With "wicked hands" (Acts 2:23) they crucified Him. But now all is over. Man has done his worst. The Cross has been endured: the appointed work is finished.

Voluntarily had the Saviour delivered Himself into the hands of sinners, and now, voluntarily He delivers His Spirit *into the hands of the Father*. What a blessed contrast! Never again will He be in "the hands of men." Never again will He be at the mercy of the wicked. Never again will He suffer shame. Into the hands of the Father He commits Himself, and the Father will now look after His interests. We need not dwell at length on the blessed sequel. Three days later the Father raised Him from the dead. Forty days after that, the Father exalted Him high above all principalities and powers and every name that is named and set Him at His own right hand in the heavens. And there He now sits on the Father's throne (Rev. 3:21), waiting till His enemies be made His footstool. For one day, ere long, the tables shall be turned. The Father will send back the One whom the world cast out: send Him back in power and glory, send Him back to rule and reign over the whole earth with a rod of iron. Then shall the situation be reversed. When He was here before man dared to arrign Him, but then shall He sit and judge them. Once He was in *their* hands, then they shall be in *His*. Once they cried "Away with *him*," then shall He say,

"Depart from *me*." And in the meantime, He is in the Father's hands, seated on His throne, awaiting His pleasure!

"Father, into thy hands I commend my spirit: and having said thus, he gave up the ghost."

3. Here we see Christ's perfect yieldedness to God.

How blessedly He evidenced this all the way through! When His mother sought Him in Jerusalem as a boy of twelve, He said, "Wist ye not that I must be about my Father's business?" When hungered in the wilderness after a forty-days fast and the devil urged Him to make bread out of the stones, He lived by every word of God. When the mighty works that He had performed and the message He had delivered failed to move His auditors, He submitted to the One who had sent Him, saying, "I thank thee, O Father, Lord of heaven and earth, because thou hast hid these things from the wise and prudent, and hast revealed them unto babes" (Matt. 11:25). When the sisters of Lazarus sent to the Saviour to acquaint Him with the sickness of their brother, instead of hurriedly going to Bethany, He abode two days still in the place where He was, saying, "This sickness is not unto death, but for the glory of God" (John 11:4). It was not natural affection that moved Him to action, but the glory of God! His meat was to do the will of the One who sent Him. In all things He submitted Himself to the Father. See Him in the morning, "rising up a great while before day" (Mark 1:35), in order that He might be in the presence of the Father. See Him anticipating every great crisis and preparing Himself for it by pouring out His heart in supplication. See Him spending the very last hour before His arrest on His face before God. How fitly might He say, "Take my yoke upon you, and learn of me; *for I am meek and lowly in heart*." And as He had lived, so He died—yielding Himself into the hands of the Father. This was the *last* act of the dying Saviour. And how exquisitely beautiful. How thoroughly in keeping with the whole of His life! It manifested His perfect confidence in the Father. It revealed the blessed intimacy there was between them. It exhibited His absolute dependency upon God.

Truly, in all things He has left us an example. The Saviour committed His Spirit into the hands of His Father in death, because it had been in the Father's hands all through His life! Is this true of you, my reader? Have you as a *sinner* committed your spirit into the hands of God? If so, it is in safe keeping. Can you say with the apostle, "I know whom I have believed, and am persuaded that he is able to keep *that which I have committed unto him* against that day" (2 Tim. 1:12, emphasis added)? And have you as a *Christian* fully yielded yourself to God? Have you heeded that word, "I beseech you therefore, brethren, by the mercies of God, that ye present your bodies a living sacrifice, holy, acceptable to God, which is your reasonable service" (Rom. 12:1)? Are you living for the glory of Him who loved you and gave Himself for you? Are you walking in daily dependence upon Him, knowing that without *Him* you can do *nothing* (John 15:5), but learning that you *can* do *all things* through Christ that strengtheneth you (Phil. 4:13)! If your whole life is yielded up to God and death should overtake you before the Saviour returns to receive His people unto Himself, it will then be easy and *natural* for you to say, "Father, into thy hands I commend my spirit." Balaam said, "Let me die the death of the righteous" (Num. 23:10). Ah, but to die the death of the righteous, you must *live* the life of the righteous, and that consists in absolute submission to and dependency upon God.

"Father, into thy hands I commend my spirit."

4. Here we see the absolute uniqueness of the Saviour.

The Lord Jesus died as none other ever did. His life was not taken from Him; He laid it down of Himself. This was His claim: "Therefore doth my Father love me, because I lay down my life, that I might take it again. No man taketh it from me, *but I lay it down of myself.* I have power to lay it down, and

I have power to take it again" (John 10:17–18). The various proofs that Christ's life was *not* taken from Him have been set before the reader in the introduction of this book. The most convincing evidence of all was seen in the committal of His Spirit into the hands of the Father. The Lord Jesus Himself said, "Father, into thy hands *I commend* my spirit," but the Holy Spirit in describing the actual laying down of His life has employed three different expressions that bring out very forcibly the fact we are now considering and the various words used by the Spirit are most appropriate to the respective Gospels in which they are found.

In Matthew 27:50 we read, "Jesus, when he had cried again with a loud voice, yielded up the ghost." But this translation fails to bring out the proper force of the original: the meaning of the Greek is He "dismissed His Spirit." This expression is most appropriate in Matthew, which is the Kingly Gospel, presenting our Lord as "the Son of David; the King of the Jews." Such a term is beautifully suited in the Royal Gospel, for the Lord's act connotes one of *authority*, as of a king dismissing a servant.

The word used in Mark—which presents our Lord as the perfect servant—is the same as in our text—taken from Luke, the Gospel of Christ's perfect Manhood—and signifies, He "breathed out His Spirit." It was His *passive* endurance of death.

In John, which is the Gospel of Christ's Divine Glory, another word is employed by the Holy Spirit: "He bowed his head and gave up the ghost" (John 19:30), or delivered up would perhaps be more exact. Here the Saviour does not "commend" His Spirit to the Father as in the Gospel of His humanity, but in keeping with His divine glory, *as One who has full power over* it, He "delivers up" His Spirit!

Two things were necessary in order to the making of propitiation: first, a complete satisfaction must be offered to God's outraged holiness and offended justice, and this, in the case of our substitute, could only be by Him suffering the outpoured wrath of God. And this had been borne. Now there remained only the second thing, and that was for the Saviour to taste of death. "It is appointed unto men once to die, but after this the judgment" (Heb. 9:27). With the sinner, it is death first and then the judgment; with the Saviour, the order was, of course, reversed. He endured the judgment of God against our sins and then died.

The end was now reached. Perfect master of Himself, unconquered by death, He cries with a loud voice of unexhausted strength and delivers up His Spirit into the hands of His Father, and in this His uniqueness was manifested. None else ever did this or died thus. His birth was unique. His life was unique. His death also was unique. In "laying down" His life, His death was differentiated from all other deaths. He died by an act of His own volition! Who but a divine person could have done this? In a mere man it would have been suicide; but in Him it was proof of His perfection and uniqueness. He died like the Prince of Life!

"Father, into thy hands I commend my spirit."

5. Here we see the place of eternal security.

Again and again the Saviour spoke of a people that had been "given" to Him (John 6:37), and at the hour of His arrest He said, "Of them which thou gavest me have I lost none" (John 18:9). Then is it not lovely to see that in the hour of death the blessed Saviour commends them now into the safekeeping of the Father! On the Cross Christ hung as the representative of His people, and therefore we view His last act as a *representative* one. When the Lord Jesus commended *His* Spirit into the hands of His Father, He also presented *our* spirits along with His, to the Father's acceptance. Jesus Christ neither lived nor died for Himself but for believers: what He did in this last act referred to them as much as to Himself. We must look, then, on Christ as here gathering all the souls of the elect together and making a solemn tender of them, with His own Spirit, to God.

The Father's hand is the place of eternal security. Into that hand the Saviour committed His people, and there they are forever safe. Said Christ, referring to the elect, "My Father, which gave them me, is greater than all; *and no man is able to pluck them out of my Father's hand*" (John 10:29, emphasis added). Here, then, is the ground of the believer's confidence. Here is the basis of our assurance. Just as nothing could harm Noah when Jehovah's hand had secured the door of the ark, so nothing can touch the spirit of the saint that is grasped by the hand of Omnipotence. None can pluck us thence. Weak we are in ourselves, but "kept by the power of God" is the sure declaration of Holy Writ—"kept by the power of God through faith unto salvation ready to be revealed in the last time" (1 Pet. 1:5). Formal professors who seem to run well for a while may grow weary and abandon the race. Those who are moved by the fleshly excitement of a "revival meeting" endure only for a time, for they have "no root in themselves." They who rely upon the power of their own wills and resolutions, who turn over a new leaf and promise to do better, often fail, and their last state is worse than the first. Many who have been persuaded by well-meaning but ignorant advisors to "join the church" and "live the Christian life" frequently apostatize from the truth. But every spirit that has been *born again* is eternally safe in the Father's hand.

"Father, into thy hands I commend my spirit."

6. Here we see the blessedness of communion with God.

What we have reference to particularly is the fact that communion with God may be enjoyed independently of place or circumstances. The Saviour was on the Cross, surrounded by a taunting crowd, His body suffering intense agony; nevertheless, He was in fellowship with the Father! This is one of the sweetest truths brought out by our text. It is our privilege to enjoy communion with God at all times, irrespective of outward circumstances or conditions. Communion with God is by *faith*, and faith is not affected by the things of sight. No matter how unpleasant your outward lot may be, my reader, it is your unspeakable privilege to enjoy communion with God. Just as the three Hebrews enjoyed fellowship with the Lord in the midst of the fiery furnace, as Daniel did in the lions' den, as Paul and Silas did in the Philippian jail, as the Saviour did *on the Cross*, so may you wherever you are! Christ's head rested on a crown of thorns, but beneath were the Father's hands!

Does not our text teach very pointedly the blessed truth and fact of communion with the Father *in the hour of death*! Then why dread it, fellow Christian? If David under the Old Testament dispensation could say, "Yea, though I walk through the valley of the shadow of death, I will fear no evil: for thou art with me" (Ps. 23:4), why should believers *now* fear, after Christ has extracted the sting out of death! Death may be "king of terrors" to the unsaved, but to the Christian, death is simply the door that admits into the presence of the well beloved. The motions of our souls in death, as in life, turn instinctively to God. "Father, into thy hands I commend my spirit" will be *our* cry, if we are conscious. While we tabernacle here, we have no rest but in the bosom of God; and when we go hence, our expectation and earnest desires are to be *with Him*. We have cast many a longing look heavenward, but when the soul of the saved near the parting of the ways, then it throws itself into the arms of love, just as a river after many turnings and windings pours itself into the oceans. Nothing but God can satisfy our spirits in this world, and none but He can satisfy us as we go hence.

But reader, *only believers* are warranted and encouraged thus to commend their spirits into the hands of God at the dying hour; how sad is the state of *all dying unbelievers*. Their spirits too will fall into the hands of God, but this will be their misery and not their privilege. *These* will find "it is a fearful thing to fall into the hands of the living God" (Heb. 10:31). Yes, because instead of falling in the arms of love, they will fall into the hands of justice.

"Father, into thy hands I commend my spirit."

7. Here we see the heart's true haven.

If the closing utterance of the Saviour expresses the prayer of dying Christians, it shows what great value they place on their spirits. The spirit within is the precious treasure, and our main solicitude and chief care is to see it secured in safe hands. "Father, into thy hands I commend my spirit." These words, then, may be taken to express the believer's care for his soul, that *it* may be safe, whatever becomes of the body. God's saint who has come nigh to death exercises few thoughts about his body, where it shall be laid, or how it shall be disposed of; he trusts that into the hands of his friends. But as his care all along has been his soul, so he thinks of it now, and with his last breath commits it to the custody of God. It is not, "Lord Jesus, receive my body, take care of my dust"; but, "Lord Jesus, receive my spirit"—Lord, secure the jewel when the casket is broken.

And now a brief word of appeal in conclusion. My friend, you are in a world that is full of trouble. You are unable to take care of yourself in life, much less will you be able to do so in death. Life has many trials and temptations. Your soul is menaced from every side. On every hand are dangers and pitfalls. The world, the flesh, and the devil are combined against you; they are too much for *your* strength. Here, then, is the beacon of light amid the darkness. Here is the harbor of shelter from all storms. Here is the blessed canopy that protects from all the fiery darts of the evil one. Thank God there *is* a refuge from the gales of life and from the terrors of death—the Father's hands—the *heart's true haven*.

Scripture Index

Index of Authors Cited